# MARTIN'S

# Junior Writers Guide

Rodney Martin

Gardner Education Ltd.
The Old Manse
Rothiemurchus, Aviemore
Inverness-Shire
PH22 1QP
tel: 0845 230 0775  fax: 0845 230 0899
email: education@gardnereducation.com
web: www.gardnereducation.com

*MARTIN'S Junior Writers Guide*
Published by Era Publications,
220 Grange Road, Flinders Park, SA 5025 Australia

© Rodney Martin, 2006
Senior Editor: Sara White
Editors: Stephen Newitt, John Pfitzner, Jessica Rawkins, Nancy Sheldon
Art Director: Lisa James
Designer: Ann Lewis
Illustrator: Richard Dall
Computer design by Barry Wallis
Printed in China by Prolong Press Limited

**National Library of Australia Cataloguing-in-Publication data:**
Martin, R. D. (Rodney David), 1946- .
Junior writer's guide.

For primary and secondary school children.
ISBN 1 74120 249 3.

1. English language - Rhetoric - Juvenile literature.  2.
English language - Grammar - Juvenile literature.  3.
Report writing - Juvenile literature.  I. Title.

808.042

About the author
Rodney Martin, Dip T(Adv), BEd, MBA, FEA
A primary school teacher and administrator for 14 years and a curriculum developer, the author
has written children's picture books and educational publications for over 30 years. He is now
an editor and publisher responsible for internationally award-winning children's literature and
classroom resources published in over 30 countries and 19 languages other than English. His
experience as a teacher, author, publisher, and editor makes his work in this *Junior Writers Guide*
practical and relevant.

Acknowledgements
For their kind permission for the use of extracts in the writing samples, the author and the
publisher wish to thank Josephine Croser and David Kennett for *Baleen* (p 11); Janeen Brian,
Lisa Herriman and Lesley Scholes for *The Fox and the Old Lion* from *Fables* (p 24); Josephine
Croser and Katharine Stafford for *Day of the Storm* (p 25); Amanda Graham for the cover of *Alex
and the Glass Slipper* (p 188).

For worldwide distribution details of
this book see the Era Publications website:
**www.erapublications.com**

| 15 | 14 | 13 | 12 | 11 | 10 | 9 | 8 | 7 | 6 | 5 | 4 | 3 | 2 | 1 |
|----|----|----|----|----|----|----|----|----|----|----|----|----|----|----|
| 15 | 14 | 13 | 12 | 11 | 10 | 09 | 08 | 07 | 06 | | | | | |

# Introduction

Writing is one of the most important things humans have invented. It enables people to pass on their ideas and thoughts to others in any place and at any time. We can learn about how the Egyptians lived thousands of years ago by reading what they wrote. Today, you can send your thoughts to people all over the world in just a few seconds by email.

Authors and editors use three special tools to help them when they write: dictionary, thesaurus and style guide. This book is a style guide.

A style guide shows how language is used in writing. It describes different kinds of writing and gives examples. It explains abbreviations, capital letters, grammar, and punctuation. It tells you how to use words that can be confusing.

In this style guide, the information is organised in sections called 'entries'. Each entry has a red headword. The headwords are in the order of the alphabet, like a dictionary, so they are easy to find.

Sometimes you find information under a headword for a *single* topic. For example, the red headword **semicolon (;)** gives you information about how to use this one punctuation mark.

Sometimes you find information under a headword for a *general* topic. For example, the red headword **punctuation** gives you information about all the punctuation marks. You will also find *semicolon* under this headword.

Sometimes there is more information about a topic in another part of the *Junior Writers Guide*. Pink cross-references tell you where to look. For example:

# limerick

A limerick is a special type of funny poem.
To find out how to write a limerick, see humour.

Your style guide is particularly useful when you are revising and editing your writing. I keep my style guide by my side during all my writing projects.

*Rodney Martin*

# a, an

The words *a* and *an* point to other words. They are always used to begin word groups (phrases).

> **a** toy　　　　**an old** toy

### When to use 'a'

Use *a* when the next word begins with a consonant sound. (This means any sound *except a, e, i, o* or *u*.)

> **a b**oy　　　　**a sh**irt

The words *boy* and *shirt* begin with the consonant sounds /b/ and /sh/.

### When to use 'an'

Use *an* when the next word begins with a vowel sound (*a, e, i, o, u*). It is hard to say two vowel sounds together (*a apple, a egg*). It is easier to say

> **an a**pple　**an e**gg　**an i**tch　**an o**range　**an u**ncle

### Beware!

The letter *h* has no sound at the beginning of some words (*honest, hour*). So words like these begin with a vowel sound.

- Use *an* (**an** hour) with these words.
  We waited for **an hour**.

The letter *u* sometimes has a consonant /y/ sound, as in *yellow* (*uniform, university, union, unit, UFO*).

- Use *a* (**a** uniform) with these words.
  The soldier wore **a uniform**.

If you want to know more, look up consonants, silent letters, vowels and WORD HISTORIES: hour.

# a, the

The words *a* and *the* point to other words. They are used to begin word groups (phrases).

> **a** tree
> **the** tall, green tree

### When to use 'a'

Use the word *a* when you mean something in general — not something definite or particular.

> I painted **a** picture.

This sentence could be about *any* picture, not a particular picture. You wouldn't know which picture the person painted.

### When to use 'the'

Use the word *the* when you mean a particular thing.

> I painted **the** picture.

In this sentence, the writer is speaking about a *particular* picture, not just any picture.

The words *this*, *that*, *these* and *those* are also used to point to or introduce other words. They all point to particular things.

> I painted **that** picture first and **this** picture second.

For more about these words, look up **articles** and WORD HISTORIES: **the**.

# abbreviations

Abbreviations are shortened forms of words and phrases. They save writers time and space.

Abbreviations are often used in addresses, emails and nonfiction writing, but not often in stories.

There are different kinds of abbreviations. Here are some examples:

*Dr* (Doctor), *Tue* (Tuesday), *Ave* (Avenue),
*PS* (Post script), *@* (at), *fax* (facsimile),
*I'm* (I am), *UFO* (Unidentified Flying Object)

## Full stops in abbreviations

Some writers use a full stop at the end of each part of an abbreviation.

**Dr. C. B.** Roberts works for the **R.S.P.C.A.**

Some writers do not use full stops in abbreviations.

**Dr C B** Roberts works for the **RSPCA**.

The modern trend is to use full stops only when the meaning is not clear.

For more information about different kinds of abbreviations, look up **acronyms**, **contractions**, **initials**, **shortened words**, **symbols** and **titles**.

## Writer's Tip

Use abbreviations only when you are sure the reader will understand them.

## Abbreviations in letter writing

In letter writing, abbreviations are used in addresses, dates, greetings, the body of a letter and the signature. Here is how an address might be written:

**Mr & Mrs P** Koh
**Apt** 2, 13 Seaside **St**
BEACHPORT **SA** 55555

(Turn the page for more about abbreviations.→)

# Abbreviations often used in letters

| | | |
|---|---|---|
| **am** (before midday) | **etc** (and so on) | **Oct** (October) |
| **Apr** (April) | **Feb** (February) | **p** (page) |
| **Apt** (Apartment) | **Fri** (Friday) | **Pk** (Park) |
| **Attn** or **Att** (Attention) | **fwd** (forward) | **pm** (after midday) |
| **Aug** (August) | **Gdns** (Gardens) | **PO** (Post Office) |
| **Ave** or **Av** (Avenue) | **Hwy** (Highway) | **POB** (Post Office Box) |
| **Bldg** (Building) | **ie** (that is) | **PS** (after writing) |
| **Blvd** (Boulevard) | **Jan** (January) | **R** (River) |
| **Capt** or **Cpt** (Captain) | **Jun** (June) | **Rd** (Road) |
| **cc** (carbon copy) | **Jul** (July) | **RSVP** (please reply) |
| **Cnr** (Corner) | **L** (Lake) | **S** (South) |
| **Cntr** (Centre) | **Ln** (Lane) | **Sat** (Saturday) |
| **Co** or **Coy** (Company) | **Ltd** (Limited) | **Sep** (September) |
| **Cres** or **Cr** (Crescent) | **Mar** (March) | **Squ** or **Sq** (Square) |
| **Crk** or **Ck** (Creek) | **Mon** (Monday) | **Sun** (Sunday) |
| **Crt** (Court) | **Mr** (Mister) | **Tce** (Terrace) |
| **Ct** or **Cct** (Circuit) | **Mrs** (Missus) | **Thu** (Thursday) |
| **Dec** (December) | **Mt** (Mount) | **Tue** (Tuesday) |
| **Dr** (Doctor, Drive) | **N** (North) | **W** (West) |
| **E** (East) | **No** (number) | **Wed** (Wednesday) |
| **eg** (for example) | **Nov** (November) | **Xmas** (Christmas) |

# Abbreviations in measures and numbers

a b c d e f g h i j k l m n o p q r s t u v w x y z

| | | |
|---|---|---|
| **1st** (first) | **F** (Fahrenheit) | **lb** (pound/s weight) |
| **2nd** (second) | **ft** (foot, feet) | **m** (metre/s; million) |
| **3rd** (third) | **g** (gram/s) | **mi** (mile/s) |
| **4th** (fourth) | **h** (hour/s) | **min** (minute/s) |
| **AD** (*anno domini* — in the year of our Lord) | **in** (inch/es) | **mm** (millimetre/s) |
| **amt** (amount) | **kb** (kilobyte/s) | **mph** (miles per hour) |
| **approx** (approximately) | **kg** (kilogram/s) | **s** or **sec** (second/s) |
| **BC** (before Christ) | **km** (kilometre/s) | **t** (tonne/s, ton/s) |
| **BCE** (before the common era) | **kph** (kilometres per hour) | **temp** (temperature) |
| **C** (Celsius) | **kW** (kilowatt/s) | **yd** (yard/s) |
| **cm** (centimetre/s) | **L** (litre/s) | **y** or **yr** (year) |

To find out where some abbreviations and symbols came from, look up WORD HISTORIES: @, am (a.m.), ampersand (&), pm (p.m.) and RSVP.

**accept** See **confusing words**: accept, except.

# acronyms

Acronyms are a kind of abbreviation. They are words made by joining the first letters or parts of other words.

The acronym *NASA* was made from the first letters of the words **N**ational **A**eronautics and **S**pace **A**dministration.

**List of acronyms**
- **Anzac** (Australian and New Zealand Army Corps)
- **CD** (compact disk)
- **DJ** (disc jockey)
- **DVD** (Digital Video Disk)
- **NASA** (National Aeronautics and Space Administration)
- **Qantas** (Queensland and Northern Territory Aerial Services)
- **radar** (radio detection and ranging)
- **RSVP** (*Répondez s'il vous plaît*)
- **SA** (South Africa, South Australia)
- **scuba** (self-contained underwater breathing apparatus)
- **TV** (television)
- **UFO** (Unidentified Flying Object)
- **UK** (United Kingdom)
- **UN** (United Nations)
- **USA** (United States of America)
- **WHO** (World Health Organisation)
- **www** (World Wide Web)

See also abbreviations and WORD HISTORIES: abbreviation, acronym and RSVP.

# addresses on letters

An address on a letter or envelope needs to have:

- the title and name of the person (*Ms E Tropez*)
- street number and name (*14 Green St*)
- suburb, town or city (*SMITHVILLE*)
- state, province, shire or region (*VIC*)
- postcode (*5555*)

Sender:
S Smart
24 Longa Ave
SPRINGFIELD WA 05555

Ms E Tropez
14 Green St
SMITHVILLE VIC 5555

Modern post offices have machines to sort the mail. It is easier for these machines to read addresses if you:

- do not use punctuation (full stops and commas)
- use capital letters for the city and state (SMITHVILLE VIC)
- always use the postcode (5555)
- write your own address at the top-left corner or on the back of the envelope

Words are often shortened in business addresses to save time and space.

Smith **& Black Co Ltd**
Smith **Bros & Assoc Ltd**

For more information, see also abbreviations.

# adjectives

Adjectives are words that give information about nouns or pronouns. They describe things.

Dogs came into the garden.

This sentence tells you nothing about the dogs.

**Two big**, **brown**, **angry** dogs came into the garden.

In this sentence the adjectives *two*, *big*, *brown* and *angry* describe the number, size, colour and mood of the dogs.

Adjectives are useful when you want to describe characters or settings for a story. In the next example, the author has not used adjectives to describe the character or the setting.

A man walked down the street at night. The moon came out from behind the clouds and its light made shadows across the road.

See what a difference the adjectives make to the picture you see in your head when you read this description of the same scene.

A **thin**, **bent** man walked down the **quiet**, **empty** street at night. The **full** moon came out from behind the **heavy**, **black** clouds and its **bright** light made **long**, **dark** shadows across the **wet**, **stony** road.

Notice that the author used each adjective once only.

**Use adjectives to compare things**

You can use adjectives to compare things. You can compare two things by adding the ending *-er* to an adjective.

Akira has **longer** hair than Olivia.

The adjective *longer* compares Akira's hair to Olivia's.

You can compare more than two things by adding the ending *-est* to an adjective.

Lina has the **longest** hair in the class.

In this example, the adjective *longest* compares Lina's hair to the hair of all the other people in the class.

**Beware!**

When you add *-er* and *-est* to adjectives that end with the letter *y*, you change the *y* to *i* then add *-er* or *-est*.

sill**y**, sill**ier**, sill**iest**    hungr**y**, hungr**ier**, hungr**iest**

The words *more* and *most* are used before some adjectives to compare things. This usually happens with long adjectives such as *difficult*.

The spelling test was **difficult**.

The writing test was **more difficult** than the spelling test.

The singing test was the **most difficult** of all tests.

Some adjectives change to different words when you use them to compare things. One example of this is *good*, *better* and *best*.

Jim is a **good** swimmer.

Jenny is a **better** swimmer than Jim.

Juanita is the **best** swimmer in the class.

Other examples like this are:

*bad*, **worse**, **worst**    *many*, **more**, **most**

Some adjectives cannot be used to compare things. One example is the adjective *full*.

The glass is **full**.

Another glass cannot be 'fuller' or 'fullest'. If something is full, then you cannot fit any more in. Other examples of adjectives like this are:

*bottom*, *top*, *empty*, *first*, *last*

To find out more about adjectives that compare, look up comparing and suffixes.

# adventure stories

Adventure stories are narratives that have lots of action and excitement. People like to read them because they can imagine they are in the story with the characters doing exciting things.

There are many kinds of adventure stories. Mysteries, science fiction, hero tales, fantasy and historical fiction can all take readers on imaginary adventures.

### Writer's tip

Here are some hints about how you can make your adventure stories exciting.

### • The character's feelings

The reader thinks about and feels what your main character is doing and feeling. If your main character is scared or bold, then the reader also feels scared or bold. So make sure your main character gets into some situations that are dangerous, scary and challenging.

### • Sentences

When very exciting things happen to your main character, use some long sentences. This makes the reader feel that a lot of things are happening all at once.

When your story gets scary for your character, use some short sentences. It creates a feeling of drama.

### • Verbs

Use action verbs (*wrestle*, *moved*, *searching*, *conquer*, *killed*, *hunted*, *raged*, *rushed*, *grappled*, *thrashed*, *tightened*, *twisted*, *turned*). This makes the story sound action-packed and exciting.

Here is an extract from a book about a powerful whale character. You can see how the author uses these techniques to create excitement.

## BALEEN

Baleen, like all whales of that time, was a predator. But Baleen was fierce and greedy beyond his need. Nothing pleased him more than to wrestle with his prey. When the battle was over, he would gloat with a new song of pride that *he* was the strongest of all.

Baleen moved through the water like a huge black shadow, searching for creatures to conquer.

First of all he killed and ate the largest fish of the seas. Then he hunted the giant squid. A mighty battle raged, as the two monsters grappled and thrashed in the water. The squid tightened its tentacles around the whale, whilst Baleen twisted and turned until he could use his long, pointed teeth upon the squid.

# adverbs

Adverbs are words that give information about verbs. They tell *how*, *when*, *where* or *how much* something happens. Many adverbs end with *-ly*.

### Adverbs that tell 'how'

The rabbit **quickly** ran into its burrow.

In this sentence, the adverb *quickly* tells *how* the rabbit ran. It gives information about the verb *ran*.

Here are some other adverbs that tell how:

*happily, sadly, well, badly, poorly, hopefully, easily, lazily, slowly, softly, loudly, heavily, quietly, sneakily*

### Adverbs that tell 'when'

The tree fell **yesterday**.

In this sentence, the adverb *yesterday* tells *when* the tree fell. It gives information about the verb *fell*.

Here are some other adverbs that tell when:

*ever, often, usually, soon, today, tomorrow, now, later, immediately, tonight, always*

### Adverbs that tell 'where'

The rabbit ran **away**.

In this example, the adverb *away* tells *where* the rabbit ran.

Here are some other adverbs that tell where:

*here, there, everywhere, outside, nearby, upwards*

### Adverbs that tell 'how much'

The fox **nearly** caught the rabbit.

In this sentence, the adverb *nearly* tells *how much* the fox caught the rabbit. It gives information about the verb *caught*.

The sentence would have a different meaning if you used another adverb instead of *nearly*.

The fox **definitely** caught the rabbit.

In this sentence, the adverb *definitely* means the fox caught the rabbit. In the first example, the fox did not catch the rabbit.

Here are some other adverbs that tell how much:

> *almost, just, slightly, only, hardly, completely, really, much, even, quite, very, extremely, totally*

## Use adverbs to compare

Adverbs can be used to compare.

> Alex sings **often**.
> Chris sings **more often** than Alex.
> Of the three performers, Pat sings the **most often**.

The words *more* and *most* are adverbs. They let us compare how often each person sings.

You can use the word endings *-er* and *-est* to make adverbs that compare.

> The boy moved **fast**.
> The cat moved **faster**.
> The dog moved **fastest**.

The adverbs *fast*, *faster* and *fastest* let you compare how fast the boy and the animals moved.

You can use the words *more* and *most* to compare how things happen.

> The hare **easily** beat the rabbit in the race.
> The hare **more easily** beat the tortoise.
> The hare **most easily** beat the snail.

The adverbs *more* and *most* let you compare how easily the hare beat the other animals.

## Beware!

Not all adverbs end with *-ly*. Here are some examples:

> *soon, later, never, yesterday, now, nearby*

Not all words ending with *-ly* are adverbs. In this sentence, the word *silly* is an adjective.

> I made a **silly** mistake.

# advertisement

The writer of an advertisement tries to persuade you to buy something or do something. Advertisements are in newspapers and magazines. They are also in catalogues, brochures and 'junk mail' in your letterbox or in spam on your computer. They are on TV, posters and signs at the movies. You can hear them on the radio. Advertisements are almost everywhere you go.

Whether the advertisement is to be read or listened to, someone must write the words or choose the pictures that will be used.

There are four main things an advertisement needs to do to make people buy or do something.

1. Get the **attention** of the audience
2. Give the audience **information** about the product
3. Make the audience **feel good** about the product
4. **Tell** the audience to buy the product

There are many ways to do these things.

## LOOK COOL!

Pop star, Cool Dude, wears *Slick* sneakers.

*Slick* sneakers last twice as long as other brands.

Get smart like Cool Dude.
Ask for *Slick* sneakers at your local store.

**To make you pay attention**, the writer:
- Uses an exclamation (!) so you think the product is exciting
- Uses capital letters to make the first words stand out
- Uses a command (*LOOK COOL!*) to tell you what to do and make you think the message is urgent
- Uses the word *cool* together with the name of the famous pop star, Cool Dude, so you think the product must be trendy

**To give you information**, the writer:
- Compares the product to other brands
- Tells you how long the product will last

**To make you feel good**, the writer:
- Says that the pop star, Cool Dude, wears the product

**To get you to buy the product**, the writer:
- Uses commands to tell you what to do. (These sentences begin with the action verbs *get* and *ask*.)
- Suggests you will look trendy, like Cool Dude
- Tells you that the product is in your local store

Look up **commands**, **exclamations** and **verbs**.

(Turn the page for more about advertisements. →)

a
b
c
d
e
f
g
h
i
j
k
l
m
n
o
p
q
r
s
t
u
v
w
x
y
z

15

## Can you chomp a Charlie?

Your tastebuds will have a wild party.

Chomp a Charlieburger today.
FREE FRIES with every burger!
It's a deal of a meal.

**To make you pay attention**, the writer:
- Asks a question so you think you need to answer
- Uses a funny drawing to make you laugh
- Uses capital letters for the words FREE FRIES

**To give you information** about the product:
- The picture shows you what the product looks like

**To give you good feelings** about the product:
- The advertisement tells you the product is tasty
- The advertisement tells you something is free so you think you are getting a bargain
- The writer uses the words *wild party* so you will feel happy

**To get you to remember and buy** the product, the writer:
- Uses a command to tell you what to do (*Chomp a Charlieburger today.*)
- Uses interesting sounds: **Ch**omp a **Ch**arlie; **FR**EE **FR**IES (alliteration) and d**eal** of a m**eal** (rhyme)

See **alliteration** and **rhyme** for more ideas.

**advice** See **confusing words**: advice, advise.

**advise** See **confusing words**: advice, advise.

**affect** See **confusing words**: affect, effect.

# affixes

Affixes are word parts that are added to root words. You can use affixes to change the meaning of root words and how you can use them. There are two kinds of affixes: *prefixes* and *suffixes*.

### Prefixes

Prefixes are joined to the beginning of a word.
    **un** + happy = **un**happy

In the word *unhappy*, *un-* is a prefix. It changes the meaning of the root word *happy*.

Two other prefixes are *re-* (*replay*) and *dis-* (*disagree*).

### Suffixes

Suffixes are joined to the end of a word.
    jump + **ing** = jump**ing**

In the word *jumping*, *-ing* is a suffix. It changes the way the root word *jump* would be used in a sentence.

Two other suffixes are *-ness* (*sadness*) and *-ful* (*hopeful*).

For more information, see **prefixes** and **suffixes**.

# agreement

Agreement is a word used to describe how words in a sentence must match or 'agree' to make sense. In a sentence, the subject and its verb must agree in number (singular or plural) or the sentence doesn't make sense.

A singular subject must have a singular verb. A plural subject must have a plural verb.

In the following sentence, the subject (*dogs*) is plural, but the verb (*was howling*) is singular. They do not agree.

    ✗ **The dogs was howling** at the moon.

In the following sentence, both the subject (*dogs*) and the verb (*were howling*) are plural. This means they agree, so the sentence makes sense.

    ✓ **The dogs were howling** at the moon.

In the following sentence, both the subject (*dog*) and the verb (*was howling*) are singular. They agree, so this sentence also makes sense.

    ✓ **The dog was howling** at the moon.

Here are some other examples:

    ✗ **Butterflies is** beautiful insects.
    ✓ **Butterflies are** beautiful insects.

    ✗ **They was** late for dinner.
    ✓ **They were** late for dinner.

**Beware!**

Look out for words (collective nouns) that mean a group. In this example there is only one family.

    ✗ The whole family **eat** dinner together.
    ✓ The whole family **eats** dinner together.

For more information, see collective nouns, plural, singular and subject.

**air** See **confusing words**: air, heir.

# allegory

An allegory is a story in which the author uses the characters and plot to stand for something else. The story has a hidden message. An allegory can be written as a poem or prose.

The old nursery rhyme 'Humpty Dumpty' is not really about an egg person who fell off a wall. It was written a long time ago about a king who was taken off his throne and his soldiers could not protect him.

> **HUMPTY DUMPTY**
>
> Humpty Dumpty sat on a wall.
> Humpty Dumpty had a great fall.
> All the king's horses and all the king's men
> Couldn't put Humpty together again.
>
> *Traditional*

Imagine if you wanted to write about a bully who was bothering people at school.

- You could invent a character. It might be a big dog that fights other dogs and takes their food.
- A terrible storm might make a tree branch fall on the big dog and trap it.
- The other dogs could rescue the big dog.
- The big dog can't walk anymore and it depends on the other dogs for food.

In this story plan, the big dog is the bully; the other dogs stand for other people in the school.

For more information about stories with hidden meanings, see fable and parable.

# alliteration

Alliteration is the repetition of the same beginning sound in two or more words that are next to or near each other.

> The **wind whipped** the leaves from the **willow** in just **one** day.

In this sentence, the author repeats the /w/ sound. Notice that not all the words in this alliteration begin with the letter *w*. The /w/ sound is made with the letters *w (wind, willow)*, *wh (whipped)* and *o (one)*. Alliteration is the *sounds*, not the *letters*.

Writers use alliteration to make interesting sound effects. You can see this in many advertisements. Businesses think it helps you to remember their products.

---

### *Harry's Hamburgers*
Hungry? Then hurry to Harry's for a humungous hamburger!

---

Alliteration is used in many old nursery rhymes.
> **S**ing a **s**ong of **s**ixpence,
> A pocket **f**ull of rye;
> **F**our and twenty **bl**ack**b**irds
> **B**aked in a pie.

There are many other ways writers use sounds. Look up **assonance**, **consonance**, **onomatopoeia**, **rhythm**, **rhyme** and **sibilance**.

**allowed** See **confusing words**: allowed, aloud.

**all right** See **confusing words**: all right, alright.

**aloud** See **confusing words**: allowed, aloud.

**alright** See **confusing words**: all right, alright.

**altar** See **confusing words**: altar, alter.

**alter** See **confusing words**: altar, alter.

# alternative spellings

Many words can be spelled more than one way. The spelling often depends on the country the writer is in. It is important to use only one spelling for a word in a piece of writing.

Some examples of words with different spellings are:
centre (center), realise (realize)
travelled (traveled), colour (color)

For more examples of words with alternative spellings, look up spelling.

# ambiguity

Ambiguity is writing that has more than one meaning.

This sentence is ambiguous.
We are worried about crime in our class.

Does this mean that there is crime happening in the class? Or does it mean the class is worried about crime generally?

Sometimes ambiguity can be fixed by changing the order of words in the sentence.
Our class is worried about crime.

When you proofread your writing, look for sentences that might have more than one meaning. It is a good idea to have someone else edit your writing to check for ambiguity. See writing process.

**among** See **confusing words**: among, between.

**an** See a, an and articles.

# and

*And* is a word used to connect ideas.

These sentences are about two different ideas.
> The tiger in the cage begged the man to let him out.
> The tiger promised he would not eat him.

The sentences can be connected with the word *and*.
> The tiger in the cage begged the man to let him out **and** promised he would not eat him.

It is not good to connect too many ideas in one sentence. For example:
> The tiger in the cage begged the man to let him out **and** promised he would not eat him **and** told him he would be his servant **and** said that he could be trusted **and** would be his friend forever.

Connecting this many ideas with *and* makes the writing harder to understand. It is also less interesting.

## Beginning a sentence with *and*

Many people believe that it is bad writing to begin a sentence with words like *and*, *so*, *but* and *because*.

There is no rule that says you cannot begin a sentence with *and*. Authors do it when they want to link an idea in one sentence with the beginning of the next sentence; but they don't do it too often or it would make their writing boring.

For more information about how writers connect ideas, see **conjunctions** and **connectives**.

# anecdote

An anecdote is a short, often funny, retelling of an incident. Anecdotes are a type of recount text.

In this example, a clown named 'Fritz' tells an anecdote about how he began his work as a clown.

> The first trick Fritz ever performed was a success. *"It was with a bowl of eggs. The top one was raw. I cracked it into a glass and drank it! All the other eggs were hard-boiled. Then I started to juggle the other eggs over the heads of the audience. The eggs dropped to the ground because I could not juggle. Everyone cried, 'Look out!' but were relieved to find that the eggs were hard-boiled and did not splatter."*

**Notes on style:**
- The first sentence is in the third person (*he*) because the author is writing about Fritz.
- The rest of the anecdote is in the first person (*I*) because Fritz is telling his own story.
- The verbs are in the past tense because Fritz is recalling his past.

For more information, look up point of view and recount.

23

# animal stories

Animal stories are narratives in which the author uses animals as characters. This gets the reader to see the world from an animal's point of view and understand the world in a different way.

In some animal stories, the animal characters act like humans. Many fables are examples of this.

## The Fox and the Old Lion

An old lion sent out word that he was ill and that he would like the animals and birds to visit him. Most went, but the fox did not. Finally the lion sent for him, asking why he had not come to see him. The wily fox replied, "I had planned to, but I noticed that although many tracks led into your cave, none led out."

*Don't just follow the crowd.*

**Notes on style:**
- The animals have human personalities. For example, they are clever, foolish or wily.
- The animals can speak, think and feel like humans. This is called 'personification'.

For more information about stories like this, look up **fable** and **personification**. Here are some famous stories with animal characters behaving like humans.

*The Wind in the Willows* by Kenneth Grahame
*The Tale of Peter Rabbit* by Beatrix Potter
*Black Beauty* by Anna Sewell
*Charlotte's Web* by E B White

24

In some animal stories, the author makes the animal characters behave as they do in real life. This might even be with extinct animals such as dinosaurs.

# Day of the Storm

As they walked, all the triceratops kept together, moving as a group. The little triceratops did not know about the Valley of Flowers or how to find her way there. She knew only that she must keep close to the others or terrible danger with black eyes, sharp teeth and claws could come.

And, like a shadow, danger was following them. A hunter, a tyrannosaur, was lurking to one side. He was watching for a small one to grow weak and drop back from the herd. He opened his mouth and snarled, then he moved a bit closer.

**Notes on style:**
- The animals behave as they would have in real life.
- They do not think or behave like humans.
- The author uses 'he' and 'she' for the animal characters instead of 'it'. These pronouns make them sound personal so it is easier for you to have feelings for the characters.

For more information, look up **pronouns**.

# anonymous (anon)

Many poems and stories have the word *anonymous* written next to them. This means that we do not know who the writer is. The word is often shortened to *anon*.

# antonyms

Antonyms are words that are opposite in meaning.

The following examples are prepositions, adjectives, verbs and nouns:

**Prepositions**
*in / out, up / down, over / under, to / from*
**Adjectives**
*high / low, fast / slow, new / old, bad / good*
**Verbs**
*add / subtract, love / hate, give / take, buy / sell*
**Nouns**
*life / death, summer / winter, night / day*

Most antonyms are not exactly opposite in meaning. For example, whether *big* is opposite to *small* depends on what the writer means by 'big' (*tall, heavy, fat, wide,* etc) and 'small' (*short, light, thin, narrow,* etc).

Many antonyms are formed with prefixes.
happy / **un**happy, like / **dis**like, polite / **im**polite

Authors and editors often use a thesaurus to look for synonyms and antonyms. They look for interesting words to use in their writing.

Antonyms can be used to compare and contrast things. This is useful in nonfiction reports.

The **smallest** known planet in our solar system is thought to be Charon; the **largest** is Jupiter. The planet **nearest** to the sun is Mercury, while the planet **furthest** from the sun is Pluto/Charon, a twin planet according to some experts.

Look up comparing, prefixes and synonyms.

# apostrophe (')

The apostrophe is a punctuation mark ('). We use it for two main reasons. It can show letters have been left out of a word (contractions). It can also show something belongs to a person or thing (possession).

### Apostrophe for contractions

The apostrophe is used in shortened words and phrases called *contractions*. It shows where letters have been left out of a word or phrase.

isn**'t**

*Isn't* is a contraction of the phrase *is not*. The apostrophe shows that the letter *o* was left out of the word *not*.

Here are some common contractions.

| Phrase | Contraction | Phrase | Contraction |
|--------|-------------|--------|-------------|
| are not | aren't | cannot | can't |
| did not | didn't | does not | doesn't |
| do not | don't | has not | hasn't |
| that is | that's | there is | there's |
| it is | it's | she is | she's |
| I will | I'll | they will | they'll |
| I am | I'm | they are | they're |
| I have | I've | we had | we'd |
| he had | he'd | was not | wasn't |

### Beware!

Many people confuse *its* and *it's*. See **confusing words**: it's, its for more information.

(Turn the page for more about the apostrophe. →)

### Apostrophe of possession (ownership)

The apostrophe is placed after a word to show that something or someone belongs to it. This is called the *apostrophe of possession*.

The **dog's collar** was loose.

The apostrophe shows the *collar* belongs to the *dog*.

When a word is singular, you usually write the apostrophe at the end of the word and then add *s,* even if the word already ends in an *s.*

I went to my **friend's** home to play.

In this sentence, the apostrophe is placed after the word *friend*, because the home belongs to *my friend*.

I went to **Chris's** home to play.

The apostrophe is placed after the word *Chris*, because the home belongs to *Chris*.

When a word is plural, it often ends with the letter *s.* So you usually write the apostrophe after the letter *s.*

It is the **boys'** job to clean their own rooms.

In this example, the *job* belongs to the *boys*.

When a plural word does *not* end with the letter *s*, write the apostrophe after the word and then add the letter *s*.

The **children's** rooms were a mess.

In this example, the *rooms* belong to the *children* and so the apostrophe is placed after that word. Other plural words like this are *men*, *women*, *mice*, *geese* and *teeth*.

### Beware!

Don't use the apostrophe with ordinary plurals.

✗ The **team's** played in the rain.

✓ The **teams** played in the rain.

Nothing in these sentences belongs to the *team*.

Don't use the apostrophe with possessive pronouns (*his*, *hers*, *its*, *theirs*, *yours*, *ours*).

✗ The dog chased **it's** tail.

✓ The dog chased **its** tail.

The apostrophe in *it's* makes the word mean *it is*. Possessive pronouns never have an apostrophe.

# appendix

An appendix is extra information to the main text of a book. It is placed at the back of a book.

An appendix is at the end of a book because the information would make the book too hard to read if the writer tried to fit it in the main text.

# argument

In an argument, a writer gives an opinion on a topic and gives reasons for the reader to believe or agree with that opinion.

Argument texts can be found in many places. They might be a letter to the editor in a newspaper, an advertisement, an essay or a discussion. In each of these types of writing, the author puts a point of view on a topic and gives reasons for or against that point of view.

There are three main parts in an argument:

**1. Introduction**
Describe the topic, give some background information and give your opinion on the topic.

**2. Argument**
Give reasons and evidence to make people believe your opinion.

**3. Conclusion**
Give a summary of your argument. Briefly remind the reader of your opinion and reasons.

(Turn the page for an example of an argument. →)

**The Perfect Gift for a Child**

The perfect gift for a child is a telescope. It can bring distant worlds into your own home. And it costs nothing to gaze at the night sky!

To the naked eye, the moon is just a disk in the sky. A telescope takes you into its craters and mountains.

Not every light in the night sky is a star. Some lights are really planets in our solar system. A telescope shows you Saturn's rings and Jupiter's moons.

Give children a telescope and you give them a journey to exciting discoveries. And there are enough lights in the night sky to keep anyone gazing for life!

- **Introduction**

The topic of this argument is 'The perfect gift for a child'. The opinion of the writer is that a telescope is the perfect gift. The background information explains what a telescope can do.

- **Argument**

The writer gives two arguments for the point of view:
1. You can see interesting things on the moon.
2. You can see planets.

- **Conclusion**

The summary reminds the reader of the ideas in the introduction and the arguments.

> **Letter to the Editor**
> **Water is gold!**
> Every day I see people wasting water as if it is worth nothing. This terrible waste should be stopped.
> People place a lot of value on gold, but gold is something we can live without. Humans cannot live without water, so that makes it more important than gold.
> I see people watering their lawns so much that the water runs down the drains where it is wasted. They could use this water to grow fruit trees or vegetables.
> The government should make water as expensive as gold. Then people would use it wisely.
> **Ms I Goldwater, Hope Valley**

- **Introduction**

The heading names the topic of the argument. In the first paragraph, the writer gives an opinion on the topic (that people should not waste water).

- **Argument**

In the second and third paragraphs, the author gives reasons and suggestions to support the opinion.

- **Conclusion**

The author reminds the reader of the topic and sums up the argument. The name of the writer is at the end.

**Notes on style:**
- Letters to the editor are usually short.
- The writer often uses the pronoun *I*, because the writing is a personal opinion.
- The writer uses the word *should* in the conclusion to say what *ought to* happen.

For more examples, look up advertisement, discussion, journalism and pronouns.

# articles

Articles are short words that introduce nouns or noun phrases. For example, the word *the* in the phrase *the brown dog* is an article.

There are two kinds of articles — definite article (*the*) and indefinite article (*a* or *an*).

For more information on how to use articles, see **a, an** and **a, the**.

# assonance

Assonance is a sound pattern made when you use the same vowel sound in a number of words. Writers often use sound patterns, like assonance, to make their writing more interesting.

The **wind whistled** through the **limbs** of the tree. In this example, the words *wind*, *whistled* and *limbs* have the same /i/ vowel sound.

**Bert's burgers** are **superb.**
In this example, the words *Bert's*, *burgers* and *superb* all have an /er/ sound as in *her*.

There are other sound patterns you can use in your writing. Look up **alliteration**, **consonance**, **onomatopoeia**, **rhyme**, **rhythm** and **sibilance**.

# audience

All writing is for an audience. There is no sense in writing if it will not be read by someone.

Sometimes people write to themselves. This might be a reminder note or a personal diary. Most often a writer creates text for other people. It might be for a family member, friend, business person or government official.

It is important to know your audience. The audience you are writing for makes a difference to the kind of language you use. Here is a movie review written to two different audiences.

### Note to a friend

> The movie 'Monster World' stinks. I think the violence is wrong for kids, the story is all over the place like a dog's breakfast and the ending is stupid. Don't waste your time or your loot.

### Review for a school paper

> The movie 'Monster World' is disappointing. In my opinion, the violence is inappropriate for children, the story does not make sense and the ending is not satisfying. I do not recommend this movie.

### Notes on style:

- In the first example, the language is informal because the writer knows the audience well.
- In the second example, the language is formal because the audience is not so private.
- The writer uses words and phrases like *I think*, *In my opinion* and *I do not recommend* to express opinions.

For more information, see formal/informal writing.

a
b
c
d
e
f
g
h
i
j
k
l
m
n
o
p
q
r
s
t
u
v
w
x
y
z

# autobiography

An autobiography is a person's life story written by that person. Autobiographies give first-hand information about people and the events in their lives.

Here is a very short example.

### A Pioneer Life

I was born on a farm in the spring of 1940. At that time, there was no electricity or other modern convenience in our part of the world. Life was tough.

My family lived far away from any school. So my school lessons were over a radio. I had to power it by pushing on pedals to turn a small electricity generator. I had one lesson per day.

There was no other child on the farm, so my only companion was a pet dog, Scrubber. He was a very clever sheepdog, so we had great fun.

I wrote to children on farms far away and talked to them over the school radio. I had to invent my own games. I think this is how I learned to invent ideas for stories. I was never bored.

**Notes on style:**

- The writing is in the first person (*I*, *my*) because it is from the point of view of the writer.
- The verbs are in the past tense (*was*, *lived*) because the author talks about past events.
- The information is in the order in which things happened (*chronological order*).

See also order, point of view, tense and WORD HISTORIES: autobiography.

**ball** See **confusing words**: ball, bawl.

34

# ballad

A ballad is a poem or song that tells a story, often about sadness, love, adventure or heroism.

Here is part of a famous old ballad about a bold fox who raids a poultry farm.

*Ballad of the Fox*

A fox went out one chilly night,
And he begged of the moon to give him light
For he'd a long way to trot that night
Before he could reach his den, O.

At first he came to the farmer's fence
Where the hedge was thick and the shadows dense;
He saw the barns, and he hurried thence
All on a summer's night, O.

He took the gray goose by the sleeve.
Says he: "Madam Goose, by your gracious leave
I'll take you away, I do believe,
And carry you home to my den, O."

Then Old Mother Flipper-Flopper jumped out of bed
And out of the window she popped her head:
"John! John! the gray goose is gone,
And the fox is off to his den, O."

Then John went up to the top of the hill
And he blew a blast both loud and shrill.
Says the fox: "The music is pretty; still
I'd rather be in my den, O."                    *Anon*

To write ballads, writers often use:
- verses with four lines
- a rhyming pattern
- a strong pattern of light and heavy beats

**bare** See **confusing words**: bare, bear.

**base** See **confusing words**: base, bass.

**bass** See **confusing words**: base, bass.

a
b
c
d
e
f
g
h
i
j
k
l
m
n
o
p
q
r
s
t
u
v
w
x
y
z

**bawl** See **confusing words**: ball, bawl.

**bean** See **confusing words**: bean, been.

**bear** See **confusing words**: bare, bear.

**beat** See **confusing words**: beat, win.

**been** See **confusing words**: bean, been.

**berry** See **confusing words**: berry, bury.

**berth** See **confusing words**: berth, birth.

**between** See **confusing words**: among, between.

# between you and me

It is a mistake to write *between you and I*. In this phrase, the word *between* should always be followed by *you and me*.

Find out why the word *between* is related to the word *two*. Look up WORD HISTORIES: between and two.

# bibliography

A bibliography is a list of books an author has read to get information or quotations for a writing project. It shows the name of the author, the title of the book and the name of the publisher. Sometimes it shows the year a book was published. The bibliography is placed at the end of a piece of writing.

For information about using other people's books when you are writing, see plagiarism, **quotation marks ("")**: Words that are quoted and reference texts.

# biography

A biography is the story of a person's life, written by another person. The information in a biography is about events that really happened. It is a kind of recount text.

Biographies help us to learn from other people's lives, especially people who did great things.

Find out why the word *biography* is related to the word *life*. See WORD HISTORIES: biography.

To write a biography, it is best if the author can interview the person the book is about. If the person is dead, then the author can interview people who knew the person or find information in the person's diaries and letters to other people.

**Notes on style:**
- Biographies are usually written in the past tense.
- The information is usually organised in order of the date or time that it happened.
- They are usually written in the third person — using the pronouns *he*, *she*, *they*.

See also autobiography, pronouns and tense.

**birth** See **confusing words**: berth, birth.

# block letters

Block letters are capital letters used for every letter in a word. They are used mainly for filling out forms. This is because block letters are easier to read in handwriting than lower-case letters.

> NAME:  MARIA LOPEZ
> ADDRESS: 13 ROMA DRIVE, ALBANY
> TOPIC:  I AM APPLYING FOR A LICENCE FOR MY DOG.

**borrow** See **confusing words**: borrow, lend, loan.

**bough** See **confusing words**: bough, bow.

**bought** See **confusing words**: bought, brought.

**bow** See **confusing words**: bough, bow.

**boy** See **confusing words**: boy, buoy.

# brackets ( )

Brackets are used in writing to surround words in a sentence. They are also called 'parentheses'. Brackets are used in several ways.

### Adding information

Brackets are used to add extra information to a sentence. Read this sentence without the words in brackets. The meaning does not change. The words in brackets just add information to the sentence.

My dog **(a border collie)** fetches the ball.

### Numbered lists

Brackets are used in numbered or alphabet lists.
Depending on your destination, the methods of passenger travel, in order of speed, are **(1)** plane, **(2)** train, **(3)** car and **(4)** ship.

Sometimes, in a list, only one round bracket is used.

> The most popular types of fiction at the library were:
> **a)** adventure
> **b)** mystery
> **c)** humour

### Play scripts

Brackets are used in play scripts to show actions.
**(The giant sees Jack as he is leaving.)**
Giant: **(angrily)** You stole my golden egg!
Jack: **(quietly)** I was only admiring it.

# brainstorming

Brainstorming is a way to gather ideas on a topic before you begin writing. It can be done by one person working alone, but it is better with a small group of people so more ideas can be gathered.

The group agrees on the topic to be brainstormed. The members of the group then share and list their ideas.

Brainstorming works best if the people in the group understand and follow some rules, such as:
- Do not discuss or explain ideas; just list them.
- Treat every idea as possibly a good idea.
- Use other people's ideas to think of more ideas.
- Do not stop to explain ideas.
- Have a time limit for the brainstorming.
- Use a recorder or notepads to jot down ideas so you don't forget them.

After the brainstorming session, it pays to sort or group the ideas under headings — main ideas, detailed ideas. Organising ideas in this way makes it easier to think about how you might begin your writing draft.

To find more information about the different stages of writing, look up writing process.

**brake** See **confusing words**: brake, break.

**break** See **confusing words**: brake, break.

**breath** See **confusing words**: breath, breathe.

**breathe** See **confusing words**: breath, breathe.

**bring** See **confusing words**: bring, take.

**brought** See **confusing words**: bought, brought.

# bullet points (•)

Bullet points (also called *dot points*) are dots or marks that are used to list items in a text. The list is usually introduced by a short sentence or phrase.

**When playing in the sun, you should:**
• Slip on a top that covers your body
• Slop sunscreen on your uncovered skin
• Slap on a hat to shade your face

**Notes on style:**
• A colon is often used at the end of the introduction line.
• A bullet point is placed at the beginning of each item in the list.

For more about using bullet points, look up lists.

**buoy** See **confusing words**: boy, buoy.

**bury** See **confusing words**: berry, bury.

# but

*But* is a word used for linking ideas in writing. It is called a *conjunction* or a *connective*.

> They set up the telescope. The night was too cloudy for viewing the stars.

Although these two sentences are about the same topic, they do not seem to be connected. The word *but* can be used to connect the ideas.

> They set up the telescope, **but** the night was too cloudy for viewing the stars.

You can begin a sentence with the word *but*; this is not wrong. However, it is not a good idea to do this too often in one piece of writing.

Look up **and**, **conjunctions** and **connectives**.

# callout

*Callout* is another name for *speech balloon* or *speech bubble*. Callouts show what characters in a text are saying or thinking.

Callouts are also used to show thoughts. Instead of a 'tail' pointing to the speaker, thoughts have a line of little 'bubbles' leading to the speaker.

Writers use callouts in comic strips and cartoons.

You can create callouts in your writing when you use a word processor. Callouts are listed under a button called 'Auto shapes'.

To see examples of speech, look up **dialogue**, **play script**, **quotation marks** (" ") and **speech**.

**can** See **confusing words**: **can, may**.

# capital letters

Capital letters are the larger form of letters. For example, the *A* is the capital of the first letter in the alphabet. Capital letters are also called *upper-case* letters. The small letters are called *lower-case* letters.

Here are the capital or upper-case letters of the alphabet.

A B C D E F G H I J K L M
N O P Q R S T U V W X Y Z

To find out why capital letters are called *upper-case* letters, look up WORD HISTORIES: upper case.

### Beginning of a sentence

The first word of a sentence begins with a capital letter.
**A** frog begins its life as an egg. **Then** it hatches from the egg as a tadpole. **Finally** the tadpole grows legs and loses its tail. **It** becomes a frog.

### First word of speech

A capital letter is used for the first word of each sentence in direct speech.
"**Monkeys** live in trees," said the zookeeper.
Dad said, "**Let's** go to the movies."

### Headings and subheadings

Headings and subheadings have capital letters. Newspaper headlines often have all letters as capitals.

---

### WHALES SEEN NEAR BEACH

About thirty whales were seen off a local beach yesterday for about four hours.

Tourists rushed to the beach to see the huge mammals swim close to the shore.

---

Words in headings and subheadings of information texts begin with capital letters.

---

**WHALES**

There are two main kinds of whales — toothed whales and baleen whales.

**Baleen Whales**

There are only eleven species of baleen whales.

---

## Poems and verse

The first word in each line of a poem or verse often begins with a capital letter.

---

**Hickory** dickory dock,
**The** mouse ran up the clock.
**The** clock struck one;
**The** mouse fell down,
**Hickory** dickory dock.

---

## Proper nouns

The special names of people, titles, places, pets and organisations begin with a capital letter.

*People*: **R**oberto **R**omano, **J**uanita **P**erez

*Titles*: **M**r Roberto Romano, **D**r Juanita Perez

*Geographical names*: **S**pringfield, **A**delaide, **N**ew **Y**ork, **C**alifornia, **U**nited **K**ingdom, **J**acob's **C**reek, **N**ile **R**iver, **M**ount **E**verest, **P**acific **O**cean, **A**ntarctica

*Pets*: **F**ido the dog

*Organisations*: **J**o's **P**et **S**tore, **U**nited **N**ations

## Time and dates

Many words to do with dates and calendars begin with a capital letter.

Her birthday is on the first **Monday** in **May**.
**New Year's Day** is the first of **January**.

(Turn the page for more about capitals.→)

a
b
c
d
e
f
g
h
i
j
k
l
m
n
o
p
q
r
s
t
u
v
w
x
y
z

**Titles of creative works**

The titles of books, plays, movies, songs, magazines and newspapers have capital letters for the main words in the title.

Her favourite book was ***An Atlas of Space Travel***.

His favourite movie is called ***Heroes***.

The **Mona Lisa**, a famous painting, is in France.

Juana recited the poem '**The Cats of Kilkenny**'.

For more information about capital letters, look up acronyms, block letters, captions and proper nouns.

# captions

A caption is a phrase or sentence that explains a picture, diagram or chart. They are used more often in nonfiction texts.

Captions always begin with a capital letter. If a caption is a full sentence, then it can end with a full stop — but this is not always done.

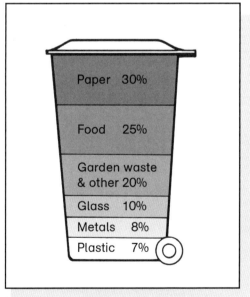

Paper   30%

Food   25%

Garden waste & other 20%

Glass   10%

Metals   8%

Plastic   7%

**What we waste in our homes**

# case

Nouns and pronouns are used in different ways in a sentence. These different uses are called *cases*. Nouns and pronouns have three cases — *subjective*, *objective* and *possessive*. You need to make sure that you use the cases properly in writing so your sentences will make sense.

**Noun cases**

Here is an example showing nouns in the different cases:

**Jennifer** ate **Jacob's sandwich**.

*Jennifer* is the subject of the sentence. She is the person the sentence is about. So the noun *Jennifer* is in the *subjective case*.

*Sandwich* is the thing that Jennifer ate. So the noun *sandwich* is in the *objective case*.

*Jacob's* is the noun that shows who owns the sandwich. So the noun *Jacob's* is in the *possessive case*. We use the apostrophe (') to show the possessive case in nouns.

Nouns do not change form for the subjective and objective cases. The possessive case changes because it needs an apostrophe.

See also **apostrophe (')**.

(Turn the page for more about case. →)

## Pronoun cases

Pronouns can change form for different cases.

| Subjective | Objective | Possessive |
|------------|-----------|------------|
| I | me | my, mine |
| you | you | your, yours |
| he | him | his |
| she | her | her, hers |
| it | it | its |
| we | us | our, ours |
| they | them | their, theirs |

**I** helped my friend. (*I* is the subject.)
**My** friend helped **me**. (*My* 'owns' the friend, so *my* is the possessive and *me* is the object.)

In these examples, the different pronoun cases *I*, *me* and *my* are used to make sense in each sentence.

If the wrong case is used, then the sentence would not be correct in formal writing.

✗ **Me** friend helped me.
✓ **My** friend helped me.

✗ **Her** and I play together.
✗ **Me** and **her** play together.
✓ **She** and I play together.

You can find out more about this topic if you look up **agreement** and **prepositions**.

# cautionary tale

A cautionary tale is a narrative that warns readers what will happen if they do not behave. It teaches a lesson.

These stories are usually short. Often they are funny. They can be in prose or verse. This example is in verse.

**The Terrible Tale of Larry**

Larry would not eat his sprouts,
    He would not eat a bean.
"You'll get sick," his parents said,
    "You'll get too thin and lean."

When vegetables were served with meals,
    He locked his teeth up tight;
No matter what the doctors said,
    Young Larry wouldn't bite.

Larry shrank to paper thin,
    Just like a sheet of foil.
His parents couldn't give him hugs,
    Because they thought he'd spoil.

And so I truly tell you now,
    It gives me no delight
To say a breeze picked Larry up —
    And blew him out of sight.

So learn this lesson well, my friends:
    Eat sprouts and beans, each day,
Lest like poor Larry, you'll get ill,
    Then fade and fly away!

**Notes on style:**

- **Sounds** – Notice the alliteration (He locked his **t**eeth up **t**ight; **L**est **l**ike poor **L**arry; **f**ade and **f**ly).
- **Order** – Each verse is four lines with an ABCB rhyming pattern.
- **Point of view** – It is told by a storyteller talking about Larry in the third person (uses pronouns *he*, *him*, *his*).

**cell** See **confusing words**: cell, sell.

**cent** See **confusing words**: cent, scent, sent.

**cereal** See **confusing words**: cereal, serial.

**certain** See **confusing words**: certain, curtain.

# character

A character in a story is a person, animal or thing the writer invents. Characters act out the story, like actors on a stage. Characters must be interesting so the reader will care about them and want to read more.

### Flat characters

Flat characters are usually simple — they play a small part in most stories. You know how they will act because they are always good, like superheroes, or always bad, like wicked villains.

### Round characters

Round characters have strengths and weaknesses. You know more about how they think and act, but they can always surprise you, like a real person.

### Inventing a character

Inventing characters is an important part of preparing for writing. Here are some things to consider when you invent characters for a story:

- **appearance** Describe size, shape, hair, clothes, etc.
- **actions** How do they walk, treat other people, sit, sleep, etc? Do they have strange habits?
- **thoughts and feelings** They might be kind or greedy, angry or happy, honest or evil, etc.
- **speech** What do they say and how do they say it?

To find out about the stages in writing, see writing process.

**choose** See **confusing words**: choose, chose.

**chose** See **confusing words**: choose, chose.

# chronological order

Chronological order means 'in order of time'. This is a way of organising information or the stages of a story.

Chronological order is usually used for:
- The entries in a personal diary or a science journal
- The events in a story (anecdote, fable, fairytale)
- The information in a recount (news story, ballad)

Adverbs of time are important when you organise your writing in chronological order. Some examples are:

*in the beginning, at first, firstly, next, then, later, after, finally, at last, in the end*

For other ways to organise writing, see order.

# cinquain

A cinquain (pronounced /**sing**-kain/) is a five-line poem without rhyme. Each line has a special purpose.

**Line 1** names the topic or title of the poem.

**Line 2** describes the topic, often with adjectives.

**Line 3** is about actions, often with verbs.

**Line 4** describes the writer's feelings.

**Line 5** goes back to the topic, often with a synonym.

> Snake
> Scaly, slithery
> Hissing and squirming
> Makes me shiver inside —
> Serpent

**Notes on style:**
- **Sounds** — the author used sibilance (**S**caly, **s**lithery, hi**ss**ing, in**s**ide) to make the poem sound like a snake.

See also adjectives, synonyms and verbs.

# clauses

A clause is a group of words that has a *subject* (something the clause is about) and a *predicate* with a verb (something said about the subject).

> The parrot [subject] talked all day [predicate].

This example is a clause because it has a subject (*The parrot*) and something about the parrot, including a verb (*talked all day*).

> The talking parrot

This example is not a clause because, although it has a subject (*The talking parrot*), it does not say anything about the subject.

Some clauses make sense on their own. This is because they can be complete sentences without needing other parts. The sentence below is a clause that makes sense by itself.

> The team practised for the big game.

Some clauses do not make sense on their own. They always need another clause to complete a sentence. Here is an example.

> which would be the end of the season.

This clause does not make sense alone. However, if you join it to the clause above, it makes a complete sentence.

> The team practised for the big game, which would be the end of the season.

You can build interesting sentences by connecting clauses.

For more information about building sentences, see **conjunctions** and **phrases**.

# cliché

A cliché (pronounced /*klee-**shay**/*) is a saying that is used so often that it makes speech and writing sound boring. It is best to avoid clichés.

Here are some examples of clichés:
> keep your nose to the grindstone
> as slow as a snail
> at the crack of dawn

To find out where this interesting word came from, look up WORD HISTORIES: cliché.

**close** See **confusing words**: close.

**cloth** See **confusing words**: cloth, clothe.

**clothe** See **confusing words**: cloth, clothe.

# collective nouns

Collective nouns are words that describe groups of people, animals or things.

Here are some examples of collective nouns:
**people**: *family*, *team* (of players), *class* (of pupils)

**animals**: *herd* (of cattle), *flock* (of sheep, birds)

**things**: *pack* (of biscuits), *bunch* (of flowers)

Remember, collective nouns are about a single group even though there is more than one thing in a group. Writers often make the mistake of using a plural verb with a collective noun in a sentence, so the subject and the verb do not agree.
> ✗ The crowd **were cheering** the players.
> ✓ The crowd **was cheering** the players.

There is only one crowd. So the verb must be *was cheering*, not *were cheering*.

For more information, see agreement and **nouns**: Collective nouns (Names of groups).

A SCHOOL OF FISH

# colon (:)

A colon is a punctuation mark you use in a sentence when you add a list of details about something.

A colon is often used at the end of a clause or phrase that begins a list.

> You can reduce pollution. **For example, at the supermarket:**
> • do not buy things that have too much plastic packaging;
> • do not use plastic carry bags;
> • recycle waste plastic.

A colon is often used after the name of a character speaking in a play.

> **Tiger:** Ha-haaaaa! Now I'm going to eat you!
> **Hunter:** Oh, no! Please don't!

# comma (,)

The comma is a mark used to separate ideas in a sentence and make meaning clear.

### Clauses and phrases

The comma is used to separate clauses and phrases in a sentence.

> <u>When the alarm rang</u>, <u>I woke up</u>.

This sentence has two clauses.

> <u>At night</u>, <u>Andrea studied the stars</u>.

This sentence has a phrase (*At night*) and a clause (*Andrea studied the stars*).

### Lists

When two or more things are listed in a sentence, commas are used to separate them.

They found an **old, dusty, dented, gold** cup.

They needed **pencils, paints, brushes, paper** and **water** to paint a picture.

In the second sentence, notice there is no comma before the word *and* in the list. The word *and* takes the place of a comma to separate the last two items in the list.

### Speech

A comma is used to separate spoken words from the rest of a sentence.

**"The chick will grow fast now,"** she said.

I said**, "Please close the door."**

# commands

A command is a type of sentence. It is used to instruct or tell someone to do something. Commands often begin with an action verb.

**Turn** the light out.
**Close** the door, please.

Commands are used in procedural texts to give instructions for doing or making something.

Add the milk to the flour. Stir quickly.

Commands are used in advertisements to get the reader to take action.

Send in your coupon. Get your free sample today!

Commands can be used for a moral to a fable.

Don't tell lies.

To find out more about using commands, see advertisement, fable and procedural text.

# comparing

Comparing can be a good way of describing something. Here are some ways you can compare in your writing.

**-er, -est**

Adjectives that end with the suffix *-er* are used to compare two things.

> A rabbit has **long** hind legs. A hare has **longer** hind legs than a rabbit.

The adjective *longer* compares the hare and the rabbit so you can tell the difference between them.

Adjectives that end with the suffix *-est* are used to compare *more* than two things.

> Of the rabbit, the hare and the kangaroo, the kangaroo has the **longest** hind legs.

**more, most**

Long adjectives often need the words *more* or *most* in front of them when you want to compare things.

> **more** beautiful     **most** interesting

**Similes**

Using similes is an excellent way of comparing things.

> The kangaroo's ears moved **like a radar**.
> The hare sat **as still as a stone**.

To find out more, see adjectives, simile and suffixes.

# compound words

Compound words are words made by joining two or more other words.

> zookeeper (zoo + keeper)

> anything, anywhere, daylight, flagpole, seagull, seaweed, silkworm, sunshine, underground

Some compound words have their word parts joined by a hyphen. These are often adjectives.

> We saw a **three-day-old** giraffe at the zoo.

If you are unsure whether a compound word should have a hyphen or not, check in a dictionary.

For more information, see hyphen (-).

# confusing words

There are many words that sound alike but have different spellings and meanings. Some words have meanings that are similar but not the same. There are words that have the same spelling but different sounds and meanings. These words often confuse people.

This section lists and explains many confusing words. They are listed in alphabetical order.

## accept, except
*Accept* is a verb. It means 'to take what someone gives you' or 'to be satisfied with something'.

> Do not **accept** gifts from strangers.

> Players must **accept** the umpire's decision.

*Except* means 'not including' or 'apart from'.

> All the projects were finished **except** mine.

## advice, advise
*Advice* is a noun. It means 'helpful information'.

> The doctor gave some **advice** about health.

*Advise* is a verb. It means 'to give someone helpful information'.

> Doctors **advise** people about health.

## affect, effect
*Affect* is mainly used as a verb. It means 'to cause a change'.

> Smoking will **affect** your health.

*Effect* is usually used as a noun. It means 'a result'.

> Sugar can have a bad **effect** on your teeth.

## air, heir
These two words sound the same but have different meanings.
*Air* is what we breathe.

An *heir* is someone who inherits another person's belongings.

## allowed, aloud
*Allowed* is the past tense of the verb *to allow* which means 'to permit or let'.

> We weren't **allowed** to sleep in.

*Aloud* is an adverb. It means 'with noise' or 'noisily'.

> They read the book **aloud**.

**all right, alright**

When *all right* means 'okay', it can be spelled *all right* or *alright*. Both are correct.

>They felt **all right** (**alright**) after the test.

When *all right* means 'all is correct', it is written as two words.

>Their answers to the test were **all right**.

**altar, alter**

These two words sound the same but have different meanings.

An *altar* is a bench or table used at religious services.

*Alter* means 'to change something'.

>A tailor can **alter** clothes to make them fit.

**among, between**

Use *among* when you talk about more than two people or things.

>The dog ran **among** the sheep in the field.

Use *between* when you talk about two people or things.

>The two children had only one apple **between** them. They had eaten nothing else **between** breakfast and dinner.

Discover why the word *between* is about two things. See WORD HISTORIES: between.

**ball, bawl**

These two words sound the same but have different meanings.

>*(See next column.→)*

A *ball* is something that is thrown, kicked, hit or bounced in games. It can also be a dance.

>Cinderella went to a **ball**.

*Bawl* means to cry loudly.

>She rocked the cradle so the baby would not **bawl**.

**bare, bear**

These two words sound the same but have different meanings.

*Bare* means 'empty, uncovered, unclothed'.

>In winter, some trees are **bare** of leaves.

>The cupboard was **bare**.

*Bear* can mean 'a large furry animal or toy'.

>The polar **bear** is a carnivore.

>My little brother sleeps with his teddy **bear**.

*Bear* can mean 'to carry'.

>The truck had to **bear** the weight of the elephant.

**base, bass**

These two words sound the same but have different meanings.

*Base* means 'the bottom part of something' or 'a central place of an organisation'.

>The **base** of the jar was cracked.

>The soldiers set up their **base** camp.

*Bass* means 'the low notes in music' or 'an instrument that plays low notes'.

>Vijay played the **bass** drum.

## bean, been

*A bean* is a vegetable.

There are many kinds of **beans** — broad **beans**, haricot **beans**, green **beans** and lima **beans**.

*Been* is a past-tense form of the verb *to be*. It is used with other verbs to make a verb phrase.

She **had been waiting** at home.

## beat, win

In tennis, you can *beat* another player and *win* the game.

If they **beat** the world record, they will **win** a prize.

## berry, bury

These words sound the same but have different meanings and spelling.

A *berry* is a small, round fruit.

**Berries** can be different sizes and colours.

*Bury* means 'to cover something with dirt, rocks or other materials'.

A landslide can **bury** a village.

## berth, birth

A *berth* is a place where a ship or boat is tied up at a wharf. It can also be a place where you sleep on a ship.

*Birth* is the time when someone or something is born.

## borrow, lend, loan

*Borrow* means 'to get something on loan from someone'.

Can I **borrow** your bike for a while, please?

*Lend* means 'to let someone have something and then give it back later'. It is a verb.

Please **lend** me your bike. I'll return it in one hour.

*Loan* means 'something that someone has lent to someone'. It is a noun.

Amir asked Aaron for a **loan** of his bike.

## bough, bow

*Bough* rhymes with *now*. It means 'a tree branch'.

The **bough** broke and fell.

*Bow* rhymes with *now*. It means 'to bend forward'.

The band lined up to **bow** to the audience.

*Bow* can rhyme with *blow*. It means 'a bent stick with a string' or 'a way of tying string or a ribbon'.

The archer had a long **bow**.

She wore a **bow** in her hair.

## bought, brought

*Bought* is the past tense of *to buy*.

He **bought** many art books.

*Brought* is the past tense of *to bring*.

She **brought** a gift for me.

HINT: Think of the letters that begin each word.

bought = **b**uy

brought = **br**ing

a
b
c
d
e
f
g
h
i
j
k
l
m
n
o
p
q
r
s
t
u
v
w
x
y
z

## boy, buoy

These words sound the same but have different meanings and spellings.

*Boy* means 'a male child or youth'.

*Buoy* means 'something that floats and is used as a marker on water'.

> They threw a **buoy** to the person who had fallen into the river.

## brake, break

*Brake* can mean 'something used to stop something from moving'.

> The car **brake** did not work.

*Brake* can mean 'to slow or stop something from moving'.

> The driver began to **brake** before turning the corner.

*Break* means 'to crack or snap something into pieces'.

> If you drop the plate, you will **break** it.

## breath, breathe

*Breath* is a noun. It means 'air that is taken into the lungs'. It rhymes with *death*.

> Fatima held her **breath**.

*Breathe* is a verb. It means 'to draw air in and out'. It rhymes with *seethe*.

> She could not **breathe** in the smoky room.

## bring, take

*Bring* means 'to fetch, move, carry or transport something *towards a named place or person*'.

> Drivers **bring** goods to our school.

> **Bring** your friend here to my house.

*Take* means 'to move, lead or carry something *away to another place or person*'.

> I had to **take** my dog to the vet.

> The mother duck **takes** her ducklings for a walk.

HINT: Remember, you *bring* it *here* but *take* it *there*.

## can, may

*Can* means 'to be able to'.

> I **can** ride a horse.

*May* is a form of the verb 'might'.

> I **may** get there in time.

*May* also means 'to be allowed to'.

> You **may** borrow my book.

HINT: People often use *can* and *may* to mean the same thing. However, in more formal language, if the meaning is about being *allowed* to do something, use *may*.

> **May** I have a chocolate?

## cell, sell

These words have the same sound.

*Cell* means 'a small room used to hold someone' or 'a very small part of some living thing'.

> The prisoner was put into a **cell**.

> With a microscope you can see the **cell** of a plant.

*Sell* means 'to accept money for something'.

> She tried to **sell** her old toys.

## cent, scent, sent

These words have the same sound but different spellings and meanings.

A *cent* is one-hundredth of a dollar.

*Scent* is a perfume or smell.

*Sent* is the past tense of *send*.

## cereal, serial

*Cereal* is a seed or grain (wheat, barley, oats, rye, etc).

> My favourite breakfast **cereal** is muesli.

A *serial* is a tale that is written or performed in several parts at different times. Serials can be books, plays, movies or television programs. The word *serial* is related to the word *series*.

> Their favourite TV **serial** is on each Monday.

HINT: To find the history of these words, see WORD HISTORIES: cereal and serial.

## certain, curtain

*Certain* means 'for sure'. It is pronounced /**sir**-tun/.

> One thing was **certain**: the stranger was not to be trusted.

*Curtain* means 'a window covering'. It is pronounced /**kir**-tun/.

> The open **curtain** let in the sunshine.

HINT: How can you be *certain* it's not *curtain*? Remember, you are **cert**ain you've passed a test if you get a **cert**ificate.

## choose, chose

*Choose* is pronounced /chooze/ as in *snooze*. It means 'to select'.

> I'd like to **choose** a new book to read.

*Chose* is pronounced /choze/ as in *doze*. It is the past tense of *choose*.

> Yesterday I **chose** a new book.

## close

*Close* is pronounced and used in two different ways.

It can be an adverb meaning 'near or nearby'. It rhymes with *dose* and *gross*.

> They kept a **close** watch on the time.

It can be a verb meaning 'to shut'. It rhymes with *doze* and *those*.

> The door began to **close** with the breeze.

a
b
c
d
e
f
g
h
i
j
k
l
m
n
o
p
q
r
s
t
u
v
w
x
y
z

## cloth, clothe

*Cloth* rhymes with *moth*. It means 'cotton, woollen, silk or other material used for making clothing'.

The tailor made a jacket from the **cloth**.

*Clothe* rhymes with *loathe*. It means 'to dress; to put on clothes'.

They collected money to **clothe** children in poor countries.

## could've, could of

Writing *could of* is a common error. The correct form is *could have* or *could've*.

✗ I **could of** done that better.

✓ I **could have** done that better.

✓ I **could've** done that better.

When people say *could have*, they often pronounce it in the shortened form — *could've*. Then when they write it, they think the ending *'ve* is the word *of* — which, of course, it is not! It is *have*.

The same error is made with *should have* (*should've*) and *would have* (*would've*).

He **should've** taken a nap.

I **would've** done it myself.

Careful writers do not to use the phrase *had have* (or *had've*). The word *have* is not needed.

✗ If I **had've** hurried, I wouldn't have missed the bus.

✓ If I **had** hurried, I wouldn't have missed the bus.

## couple, few, several

*Couple* means 'two'.

The **couple** carried a heavy box between them.

He ate a **couple** of pies — one today and one yesterday.

*Few* means 'more than two, but not many'.

Eating a **few** chocolates is OK, but a whole box is too many.

She slept for a **few** hours in the afternoon.

*Several* means 'more than a few, but not many'.

There were **several** wolves in the pack.

There are **several** words that mean 'big'.

## creak, creek

These words have the same sound.

*Creak* means 'a squeaking sound often made by a door hinge'.

She oiled the door so it wouldn't **creak**.

*Creek* means 'a small stream of water'.

## currant, current

A *currant* is a dried grape.

Some cakes have **currants**.

*Current* can mean 'present, fashionable, of this time, now' or 'the flow of water, air or electricity'.

By reading newspapers you learn about **current** events.

The raft drifted with the sea **currents**.

HINT: Remember that *currant* and *grape* both have the letters *ra*.

**cymbals, symbols**

*Cymbals* are musical instruments used by a drummer or percussionist.

The percussionist in the orchestra crashed the **cymbals** together.

*Symbols* are marks or designs used instead of words.

Scientists and mathematicians use many **symbols**.

The $, £ and € are **symbols** for money in different countries.

See also symbols.

**dairy, diary**

These words are often confused because their spelling is so similar.

A **dairy** is a farm where cows are kept to produce milk.

A **diary** is a personal journal.

HINT: It's **airy** on a d**airy**.

**dear, deer**

*Dear* means 'expensive' or 'loved'.

The *deer* is a large grazing animal.

The **deer** hid among the trees.

Many **deer** gathered in a herd.

**desert, dessert**

*Desert* can mean 'a dry piece of land often covered with sand or ice'. It is pronounced /**dez**-ert/.

Antarctica is a frozen **desert**.

*Desert* can mean 'to abandon'. It is pronounced /dee-**zert**/.

The people had to **desert** their homes during the floods.

(*See next column.*→)

*Dessert* means 'something sweet eaten at the end of a meal'. It is pronounced /dee-**zert**/.

We ate ice cream for **dessert**.

HINT: You'll find more in WORD HISTORIES: dessert.

**dew, due**

These words have the same sound. *Dew* means 'the early-morning droplets of water on grass'.

*Due* means 'expected to arrive' or 'to have been done'.

I handed in my project when it was **due**.

I plane is **due** to arrive today.

**die, dye**

These words sound the same. *Die* means 'to stop living'.

Without water, plants will **die**.

*Dye* means 'to change the colour of something by using a colour stain'.

Hairdressers often **dye** people's hair different colours.

**doe, dough**

These words sound the same. They rhyme with the word *go*.

A *doe* is the female of certain animals — rabbits, deer.

*Dough* is a flour and water mixture used to bake bread and pizza.

a
b
c
d
e
f
g
h
i
j
k
l
m
n
o
p
q
r
s
t
u
v
w
x
y
z

61

**draw, drawer**

*Draw* means 'to create a picture with a pen, pencil, crayon or other drawing tool' or to 'to be equal at the end of a game'.

> Azur liked to **draw** pictures.

> Each team scored two goals, so the game was a **draw**.

A *drawer* is a storage compartment that slides in and out of a piece of furniture. The word sounds the same as *draw*.

> Jo kept her artwork in a **drawer**.

A *drawer* is also 'a person who draws'. It is pronounced /**dror**-er/.

> Jo is the **drawer** of the biggest picture on the wall.

**either, neither**

*Either* means 'one or the other'.

> **Either** Ben or Alicia knows the answer to the question.

*Neither* means 'not one nor the other'.

> **Neither** Ben nor Alicia knows the answer to the question.

**Beware!** Notice that the examples have the word *knows* and not the word *know*. The words *either* and *neither* in these examples are both singular words. This means they need a singular verb.

> ✗ **Neither** Ben nor Alice **know** the answer.

> ✓ **Neither** Ben nor Alice **knows** the answer.

For more about this, look up agreement and singular words.

**ewe, yew, you**

A *ewe* is a female sheep.

> The **ewe** gave birth to a lamb.

A *yew* is a type of tree.

> In olden days, bows were made from the wood of the **yew** tree.

*You* is a pronoun in the second (other) person.

> If **you** do this for me I will give **you** a reward.

**Beware!** The plural forms of *ewe* and *yew* are **ewes** and **yews**. The plural of *you* is **you**. Careful writers do not write or say *yous*.

**fair, fare**

*Fair* means 'an amusement show; a carnival'. It can also mean 'honest and just' or 'light coloured (hair or skin)'.

*Fare* means 'a fee for travelling on a bus, train, plane, ferry or other method of travel'.

**farther, father**

These words have the same sound. A *father* is a male parent.

> My **father** and mother watched me play tennis.

*Farther* means 'a longer distance'.

> They couldn't walk any **farther**.

**farther, further**

These words both mean 'a longer way' or 'more'.

> She swam **farther** than she had ever swum before.

> The **further** he walked, the more his feet hurt.

> I can help you no **further**.

(*See next page.*➔)

*Further* seems to be more popular than *farther* in many parts of the world when talking about distance.

## fate, fete

These words have the same sound.
*Fate* means 'your destiny; what will happen to you'.
> James did not do his homework, so his **fate** would not be pleasant.

*Fete* means 'a festival or activity to raise money for a charity'.
> They gathered clothes and toys to sell at the church **fete**.

## fewer, less

You use these words to compare 'how many' or 'how much'.

*Fewer* means 'not as many, a smaller number'. Use the word *fewer* for things you can count.
> There are **fewer** students at school today than yesterday.

*Less* means 'not as much; a smaller quantity'. Use the word *less* when you describe things you *can't* count.
> The students worked **less** in the hot weather.

## fir, fur

A *fir* is a type of tree that has thin needle-shaped leaves.
> **Fir** trees are evergreens.

*Fur* is the hairy coat covering many mammals.
> The tiger has stripes in its **fur**.

## flaw, floor

*Flaw* means 'an error; a mistake in how something was made or done'.
> The inspector found a **flaw** in the products at the factory.

*Floor* means 'the flat part of any room you walk on'.
> They swept the **floor** clean.

## flea, flee

A *flea* is an insect that sucks an animal's blood.
> The dog scratched at a **flea**.

*Flee* means 'to run from danger'.
> People had to **flee** the storm.

Here is a verse that plays with the words *flea* and *flee*.

> A **flea** and a fly in a flue,
> Were trapped so what could they do?
> Said the **flea**, "Let us fly."
> Said the fly, "Let us **flee**."
> So they flew through a flaw in the flue.
> *Anon.*

See also **confusing words**: flaw, floor and flew, flu, flue.

## flew, flu, flue

These words have the same sound but different meanings.
*Flew* is the past tense of *to fly*.
> The bird **flew** past the window.

*Flu* is short for *influenza*.
> Three people were ill with the **flu**.

A *flue* is a space where air or gases can pass.
> They cleaned the chimney **flue**.

a
b
c
d
e
f
g
h
i
j
k
l
m
n
o
p
q
r
s
t
u
v
w
x
y
z

**flour, flower**

*Flour* is the soft cooking powder made by milling or grinding wheat, rye, corn or other grain.

> Dough is a mixture of **flour** and water.

A *flower* is the blossom of any plant.

> The **flower** of a rose is beautiful, but be careful of the thorns.

**for, four**

*For* is a preposition. It is used to begin a phrase.

> I took my dog **for** a walk.

> Traffic lights were invented **for** a very good reason.

*Four* is a number.

> A square has **four** sides.

**foul, fowl**

*Foul* means 'bad; rotten'.

> A **foul** smell came from the bin.

*Fowl* means 'a chicken or other bird that is often eaten'.

> The **fowl** laid an egg each day.

**good, well**

*Good* means 'well-behaved, enjoyable'.

> The children were **good** for the babysitter.

> Everyone had a **good** time.

*Well* can mean 'properly, carefully' or 'healthy'.

> They washed the dog **well**.

> I did not feel **well** with the flu.

*Well* can also mean 'a hole in the ground to hold water'.

> The pioneer farmers dug a **well**.

(See next column. →)

The words *good* and *well* are often confused in conversation.

> Teacher: How are you, Sam?

> ✗ Sam: I'm **good**, thanks.

Sam's answer *good* means 'well-behaved'. The reply should have been

> ✓ Sam: I'm **well**, thanks.

This means he is healthy.

Writers often create jokes with words that have more than one meaning. This verse makes fun with the word *well*.

> Doctor Bell fell down a **well**
> And broke his collarbone.
> Doctors should attend the sick
> And leave the **well** alone.
> *Anon.*

**guessed, guest**

*Guessed* is a form of the verb *to guess*. It means 'to estimate something'.

> Sara **guessed** there were two hundred and ten seeds in the jar.

*Guest* means 'a person invited to a place or event'.

> One **guest** arrived late for the party.

**had've, had of**

See **confusing words**: could've, could of.

64

**hair, hare**
*Hair* is the thread-like growth that is the fur on most mammals.
> Sally's red **hair** looked great.
> Their dog leaves **hair** on the carpet when it comes inside.

*Hare* means 'a four-legged mammal that looks like a rabbit'.
> The **hare** is related to the deer.

**hanged, hung**
These words are past-tense forms of the verb *to hang.*
*Hanged* is used for people.
> In some countries, people are **hanged** for serious crimes.

*Hung* is used for things.
> They **hung** pictures on the wall.

**heal, heel, he'll**
*Heal* means 'to cure or make well'.
> Broken bones take weeks to **heal**.

*Heel* means 'the back of your foot'.
> Franco fell and twisted his **heel**.

*He'll* is the shortened form of the phrase *he will*.
> **He'll** be here soon.

**hear, here**
*Hear* means 'to take in sounds using your sense of hearing'.
> They could **hear** the bell ringing.

*Here* means 'in this place'.
> Sit **here** next to me, not over there by yourself.

HINT: You h**ear** with your **ear**s.

**heard, herd**
*Heard* is the past tense of the verb *to hear*.
> In the darkness, she **heard** a strange sound behind her.

*Herd* means 'a large group of animals such as cattle'.
> The **herd** of cattle gathered at the river to drink.

HINT: The word **hear**d has the word **hear** in it.

**him, hymn**
*Him* is a pronoun meaning 'a male'.
> Peter's friend gave **him** a gift.

*Hymn* means 'a religious song'.
> They sang a **hymn** at the church.

**hoarse, horse**
*Hoarse* means 'having a husky or rough voice'.
> Jennifer was **hoarse** from yelling at the football game.

A *horse* is a four-legged animal.
> The **horse** galloped away.

**hole, whole**
*Hole* means 'a hollow space in something'.
> Shamira drilled a **hole** in the wall to hang a picture.
> The gardener dug a **hole** in the ground.

*Whole* means 'complete; in one piece'.
> Luke ate the **whole** cake!

a
b
c
d
e
f
g
h
i
j
k
l
m
n
o
p
q
r
s
t
u
v
w
x
y
z

**hour, our**

*Hour* means 'a measure of time; sixty minutes'.

It took us one **hour** to finish the project.

*Our* is a pronoun that means 'something belongs to us'.

This poster is **our** project. We did it as a team.

**Did you know?** To find out why the word *hour* begins with a silent letter *h*, see WORD HISTORIES: hour.

**in, inn**

*In* means 'within; inside something'.

The treasure was **in** a big chest.

I will be there **in** a minute.

*Inn* means 'a small hotel where travellers stay overnight'.

The backpackers slept at an **inn**.

**it's, its**

*It's* is short for *it is*. The apostrophe shows that the letter *i* has been left out of the word *is*.

**It's** a long way to the sun.

*Its* is a form of the pronoun *it* to show that something belongs to it.

The cat licked **its** fur.

The *fur* belongs to the cat (it), so we put the letter *s* after the word *it*. We do not use an apostrophe in pronouns that show possession.

For more information, see apostrophe (').

**key, quay**

These words have the same sound. *Key* means 'something used to open a lock' or 'a button on a computer keyboard'.

The door **key** was missing.

He hit the wrong **key** and made a spelling mistake.

*Quay* means 'a platform where people load and unload boats'.

The passengers got off the ship at the **quay**.

**knew, new**

*Knew* is the past tense of *to know*.

I **knew** the answer to the quiz.

*New* means 'young, fresh, unfamiliar, recent, not old'.

I moved to a **new** school.

The supermarket put the **new** apples on display.

**knight, night**

A *knight* used to wear armour and fight in battles. Today, a knight is a man who has been given the title 'Sir' by a king or queen for doing special deeds for the country.

There are many stories about **knights** in armour.

Sir Henry Jodpur became a **knight** for his services to the community.

*Night* is the time of darkness between sunset and sunrise.

Owls hunt at **night**.

**Did you know?** To find out why the word *knight* has a silent letter *k*, see WORD HISTORIES: knight.

## knit, nit

*Knit* means 'to use long needles to loop threads of wool or other material together and make a piece of clothing or other item'.

He used red wool to **knit** a scarf.

A *nit* is the egg or young of head lice.

People can get rid of **nits** by using a special shampoo.

## knot, not

A *knot* is 'a way of tying threads together' or 'a lump on a tree'.

The truck driver tied a **knot** in the rope so the load would stay on.

The birds built a nest around a **knot** in the tree trunk.

*Not* means 'in no way'.

It is **not** a good idea to cross a road without looking for traffic.

He did **not** eat because he felt ill.

## laid, lay, lie

These words can each have more than one meaning.

*Lay* is usually used as a verb. It can mean 'to put down; to place'.

Moths **lay** their eggs and die.

We **lay** a cloth on a table.

They could not **lay** their hands on the missing books.

*Laid* is the past tense of *lay* meaning 'to put down; to place'.

Moths **laid** eggs in my clothes.

We **laid** a cloth on the table.

(*See next column.*→)

*Lie* can be a verb meaning 'to be in a flat position; to be spread out'.

I feel ill, so I will **lie** down.

*Lay* is also the past tense of the verb *to lie* meaning 'to be in a flat position'.

Yesterday I felt ill so I **lay** down.

At night, the city **lay** before us like a carpet of lights.

*Lie* can mean 'to tell an untruth'.

It is better not to **lie** to people.

*Lie* can be a noun meaning 'something that is not true'.

It is better not to tell a **lie**.

## learn, teach

*Learn* means 'to get to know and understand something'. It is about *getting* knowledge.

A dog can **learn** to fetch the ball.

I want to **learn** to play the piano.

*Teach* means 'to show or help someone to learn a skill or to know or understand something'. It is about *giving* knowledge. You cannot *learn* for others, but you can *teach* others or yourself to do something.

Tania will **teach** her dog to sit.

I can **teach** you to write a story.

You can **teach** yourself to spell.

**Beware!** We can teach someone to do something, but we don't say we learn someone to do something.

## lend

See **confusing words**: borrow, lend, loan.

a b c d e f g h i j k l m n o p q r s t u v w x y z

**liar, lyre**

These words sound the same.

A *liar* is a person who tells lies.

> People often do not trust a **liar**.

A *lyre* is an ancient stringed musical instrument.

> You might find a **lyre** in a museum of musical instruments.
> The Australian **lyre**bird got its name from the shape of its tail.

**loan**

See **confusing words**: borrow, lend, loan and loan, lone.

**loan, lone**

*Loan* means 'something that someone has lent to someone'.

> He wanted a **loan** of my bike.

*Lone* means 'by itself, himself or herself'.

> A **lone** wolf howled at the moon.

HINT: L**one** means **one**.

**loose, lose**

*Loose* means 'not tight'. It rhymes with *juice*.

> My shoelace was **loose**.

*Lose* means 'to misplace, to be beaten, to not find'. It rhymes with *snooze*.

> Keep your key on a ring so you don't **lose** it.
> The team would **lose** the game if it didn't get another goal.
> You can **lose** your way in a strange place.

**mail, male**

*Mail* is letters and parcels sent by post.

> A surprise arrived in the **mail**.

*Male* means 'a boy or man'. In other animals, it is the sex that does not have babies; the opposite of *female*.

> A **male** chicken is called a rooster.

**main, mane**

*Main* means 'the biggest; the most important'.

> The **main** road was blocked.
> The **main** cause of the accident was carelessness.

A *mane* is the long hair on the neck or head of some animals.

> Only the male lion has a **mane**.
> A zebra's **mane** stands upright.

**many, much**

*Many* means 'lots of' in number. It is used when you are talking about things that can be counted.

> How **many** dollars do I need?
> They ate too **many** chocolates.

*Much* also means 'lots of' or 'a big quantity'. It is used when you are talking about an amount that is not counted.

> I don't have **much** money.
> How **much** sugar is in the bowl?

**mare, mayor**

*Mare* means 'a female horse'.
    The **mare** gave birth to a foal.

*Mayor* means 'the leader of a town or city council'.
    The **mayor** wore special robes.

**meat, meet**

*Meat* is animal flesh used for food.
    Vegetarians do not eat **meat**.

*Meet* means 'to get together with someone; to gather in one place; to connect or join'.
    Friends often **meet** to have fun.
    Today, committees can **meet** in a room or on the telephone.
    Roads **meet** at a crossroad.

HINT: M**eat** is what you **eat**.

**medal, meddle**

A *medal* is a disk or badge given to people as a reward.
    The soldier was given a **medal**.
    Jane won a gold **medal** in the swimming competition.

*Meddle* means 'to interfere; to intrude in other people's business'.
    I use a password so no one can **meddle** with my computer.

**meter, metre**

A *meter* is an instrument for measuring things such as water, gas, distance, electricity or time.
    Your water **meter** shows how much water you have used.

A *metre* is a measure of length.
    The runners raced over a distance of one hundred **metres**.
    He is two **metres** tall.

**naval, navel**

*Naval* means 'to do with a navy'.
    Many sailors wear a **naval** uniform and work on **naval** ships.

Your *navel* is your 'belly button'.
    You can tell a **navel** orange by its belly button shape on one end.

HINT: Your nav**el** is on your b**el**ly.

**oar, or, ore**

These words all have the same sound.

An *oar* is a paddle used to row a boat.
    The **oar** broke as they rowed.

*Or* is a word used to connect ideas that are choices in a sentence.
    Do you want salad **or** pasta?
    You can eat it now **or** you can save it for later.
    Do you like juice, milk **or** water?

*Ore* means 'earth that is mined for minerals'.
    Steel is made from iron **ore**. The **ore** comes from the ground.

## of, off

These words have different sounds and different meanings.

*Of* is pronounced /ov/. It is used with other words in a phrase.

The lion is called 'king **of** beasts'.

**Of** course you can do it.

I scored ten out **of** ten in the test.

*Off* rhymes with *cough.* It means 'out of; away from; not on'.

He stepped **off** the bus.

Keep **off** the grass.

The power was **off**, so I could not do my homework.

## one, won

These words have the same sound.

*One* means 'the numeral 1'.

They had lunch at **one** o'clock.

**One** day, I will write a book.

*Won* is the past tense of *to win*.

Sally **won** a drawing competition.

## pail, pale

A *pail* is a bucket.

Jack and Jill went up the hill to fetch a **pail** of water.

*Pale* means 'not having a bright colour; looking whitish in skin colour because of illness'.

You can make a **pale** blue colour by mixing dark blue with white.

His face went **pale** as he fainted.

## pain, pane

*Pain* means 'an uncomfortable feeling such as a sting or ache'.

She felt a sharp **pain** as she fell.

*Pane* means 'a sheet of glass in a window or door'.

They washed the window **pane**.

## pair, pear

*Pair* means 'two people or things that go together; a set of two'.

Tom and Tara went as a **pair** to dancing lessons.

He used a **pair** of scissors to cut the paper.

A *pear* is a fruit that grows on a tree.

A ripe **pear** is very juicy.

## passed, past

*Passed* is a form of the verb *to pass*. It means 'to go by' or 'to hand over'.

The ambulance **passed** us on the road.

The player **passed** the ball to another team-mate.

*Past* is an adverb that tells 'where'. It can also mean 'beyond' or 'a time before now'.

The crowd rushed **past** me.

It was **past** their bedtime.

The old man kept talking about the **past**, when he was young.

**paw, poor, pore, pour**
A *paw* is the foot of an animal that has nails or claws.

    The dog had a thorn in its **paw**.

*Poor* means 'not rich; bad quality; unfortunate'.

    Some organisations collect money to help the **poor**.

    The toy had a **poor** design.

    The **poor** animal was in pain.

*Pore* means 'a tiny opening in your skin' or 'to look at something closely'.

    Through a magnifying glass you can see the **pores** in your skin.

    Jose took a long time to **pore** over every detail in the picture.

*Pour* means 'to tip something from a container' or 'to flow down in large amounts'.

    I had to **pour** the juice carefully.

    The rain began to **pour** down while we were walking.

**peace, piece**
*Peace* means 'a time when all is calm or quiet; a time without war'.

    I wanted **peace** and quiet while I read my book.

*Piece* means 'a part or section of something'.

    The dog chewed a **piece** of bone.

HINT: Remember a **pie**ce of **pie**.

**peal, peel**
*Peal* means 'the ring of a bell'.

    The **peal** of the church bells could be heard all over the town.

*Peel* means 'the skin of a fruit or vegetable' or 'to strip away the skin of a fruit or vegetable'.

    Lemon **peel** tastes bitter.

    I cry when I **peel** onions.

**plain, plane**
*Plain* means 'a big, flat area of land; simple and ordinary'.

    The cattle grazed on the grassy **plain**.

    He liked **plain** white bread.

*Plane* means 'a tool used to smooth wood; an aircraft (short for *aeroplane*)'.

    The carpenter used a **plane** to smooth the edge of the timber.

    The **plane** landed at the airport.

**practice, practise**
*Practice* means 'a rehearsal'. It is a noun.

    I have piano **practice** at eight o'clock each morning. I believe that **practice** makes perfect.

*Practise* means 'to rehearse; to do something over and over to get better at it'. It is a verb.

    I **practise** piano at eight o'clock each morning. I need to **practise** more often.

**praise, prays, preys**

*Praise* means 'positive words about someone or something'.

> The review was full of **praise** for the new movie.

*Prays* means 'speaks to God; strongly hopes'.

> A farmer **prays** for rain when the seed is planted.

*Preys* means 'hunts for food'.

> The lion **preys** on other large animals for food.

**principal, principle**

*Principal* means 'head of a school; chief or main'.

> The **principal** spoke to the class.

> The **principal** reason for the meeting was to solve a problem.

*Principle* means 'a basic rule; something you believe is right or correct'.

> People should treat others on the **principle** that honesty is best.

> I recycle plastic as a matter of **principle**.

**profit, prophet**

*Profit* means 'the money you keep when you sell something for more than you pay for it'.

> I bought an old bike for ten dollars. I sold it for fifteen dollars. My **profit** was five dollars.

*Prophet* means 'a person who says what will happen in the future; a person who says that he/she understands and speaks the wishes of a god'.

*(See next column.➜)*

Many religions have **prophets**. You can read about **prophets** in religious books.

**quiet, quite**

*Quiet* means 'silent; not loud or noisy'. It is pronounced /**kwi**-et/.

> The police asked people to remain **quiet**.

> Liu spoke **quietly** to her friend.

*Quite* means 'completely; absolutely'. It rhymes with *kite*.

> The test was **quite** easy to do.

> The artist said the painting was not **quite** finished.

**rain, reign, rein**

*Rain* is water falling from clouds in the sky.

> The **rain** was so heavy that it made the river flood.

*Reign* means 'to rule a country as a king or queen'.

> Queen Elizabeth II has **reigned** in England for many years.

*Rein* means 'a strap used by a rider to control an animal such as a horse'.

> The jockey pulled on the **reins** to stop the horse.

**raw, roar**

*Raw* means 'not cooked'.

> The steak was **raw**. All the other meat was well done.

*Roar* means 'to make a loud sound, like a lion's roar'.

> The tiger **roared**.

> Winds **roar** during a storm.

**read, red, reed**

*Read* means 'to look at and understand written words and images'. In the present tense it rhymes with *reed*; in the past tense it rhymes with *red*.

I can **read** a map.

Yesterday I **read** a book.

*Red* means 'the colour of a ripe tomato'.

The flags of several nations are coloured **red**, white and blue.

*Reed* means 'a tall, thin wetland plant'.

**Reeds** in a wetland help to clean water before it reaches the sea.

**real, really**

These words are often misused, especially by sports commentators.

*Real* describes whether something is genuine or true. It is an adjective.

It was a **real** disappointment when they lost the game.

*Really* means 'truly; in fact; very'. It is an adverb.

The footballer played **really** well.

I was **really** disappointed when they lost the game.

HINT: If you mean **very**, then use **really**. They both end with **y**.

**real, reel**

*Real* means 'genuine; factual; true'.

A biography is about a **real** person.

The bag was made of **real** leather.

(*See next column.*→)

*Reel* means 'a Scottish dance; a wheel-shaped instrument for winding things onto; to wind in'.

The dancers performed the traditional Scottish **reel**.

The fishing line became tangled around the **reel**.

She hooked the fish and began to **reel** it in.

**right, write**

*Right* means 'correct; the opposite direction of left'.

They knew the **right** answer.

Do we turn left or **right**?

*Write* means 'to use letters, words and sentences to record ideas'.

You can use a pencil, pen or computer to **write** a message.

**road, rode**

A *road* is a way that has been cleared for vehicles to travel on.

That **road** leads to a lake on the other side of the forest.

*Rode* is the past tense of *to ride*.

The cyclists **rode** for three hours.

**root, route**

*Root* means 'the part of a plant that usually spreads underground'.

The **roots** of many trees spread underground as far as their branches spread above.

*Route* means 'the directions you take to get to a place'.

The explorers had to find a **route** through the mountains.

a
b
c
d
e
f
g
h
i
j
k
l
m
n
o
p
q
r
s
t
u
v
w
x
y
z

## rung, wrung

*Rung* means 'a step on a ladder'. It is also the past tense of the verb *to ring*.

> The bottom **rung** on the ladder was broken.

> I have **rung** him twice on the phone but he did not answer.

> The church bells were **rung** at the wedding.

*Wrung* is a past-tense form of *to wring* meaning 'to twist and squeeze'.

> The water was **wrung** out of the clothes after they were washed.

## sail, sale

*Sail* means 'a strong sheet on a boat to catch the wind; to move across water on a boat'.

> The wind was so strong that it tore the **sail** and the boat could not move.

> Her favourite holiday was to **sail** on a ship.

*Sale* means 'when something is sold; a time when shops sell things at lower prices'.

> The old house was for **sale**.

> Shoes were cheap at the **sale**.

## sauce, source

*Sauce* is 'anything liquid or soft that is poured onto or mixed with food to add flavour'.

> The cook added meat **sauce** to the pasta.

(*See next column.* →)

*Source* means 'the place anything comes from'.

> The **source** of the information was a secret.

> Vegetables are a **source** of vitamins.

## saw, soar, sore

*Saw* can mean 'a tool for cutting'.
> You can cut timber with a **saw**.

*Saw* is also the past tense of *to see*.
> We **saw** the moon through a telescope.

*Soar* is a verb meaning 'to fly'.
> The eagle can **soar** on the wind.

*Sore* means 'a wound' or 'painful'.
> The **sore** took two weeks to heal.
> She has a **sore** throat.

## sea, see

*Sea* means 'a large area of salt water'.
> Ships sail across the **sea**.

*See* means 'to view with your eyes; to understand something'.
> I could **see** craters on the moon.
> I **see** what you mean.

## sew, so, sow

Each of these words rhymes with *go*.

*Sew* means 'to join cloth with stitches'.
> With a needle and cotton, I could **sew** a new button onto my shirt.

*So* can mean 'very'.
> The family was **so** hungry, twenty pizzas were not enough.

(*See next page.* →)

*So* can mean 'therefore' when you want to connect ideas in a sentence.

> We were hungry. We ate pizza.
>
> We were hungry, **so** we ate pizza.

*Sow*, when it rhymes with *go*, means 'to plant'.

> After turning the soil, the farmer had to **sow** the seeds.

*Sow* can also rhyme with *cow*. It means 'a female pig'.

> The **sow** had a litter of piglets.

## shear, sheer

*Shear* means 'to cut'.

> The farmer gathered the sheep so he could **shear** them and send their wool to the market.

*Sheer* means 'transparent; very steep; absolute; extreme'.

> The curtain was **sheer**, so you could see through it.
>
> The rock climbers got to the top of a **sheer** cliff.
>
> The children laughed with **sheer** delight at the clown.

## should've, should of

See **confusing words**: could've, could of.

## son, sun

*Son* means 'a male child in a family'.

> The Smith family had a **son** and a daughter.

The *sun* is the star in our solar system.

> The **sun** gives us light and heat.

## stair, stare

A *stair* is one of a series of steps that lead from one level to another.

> The **stairs** led down to a cellar.

*Stare* means 'to look at something for a long time'.

> The crowd **stared** at the famous pop star as she walked past.

## stake, steak

A *stake* is a pointed post that is pushed into the ground.

> Many tomato plants grow better if you tie them to a **stake**.

A *steak* is a thick slice of meat from a cow, large fish or other animal.

> The **steak** was cooked well.

## stalk, stork

*Stalk* means 'a plant stem' or 'to follow something or someone without being seen or heard'.

> The celery **stalk** was fresh.
>
> Lions **stalk** their prey.

A *stork* is a large bird with long legs and a long neck and beak.

## steal, steel

*Steal* means 'to take what is not yours without the owner's permission'.

> It is against the law to **steal**.

*Steel* is a metal made with iron and small amounts of other minerals.

> **Steel** is used in most buildings because it is very strong.

a
b
c
d
e
f
g
h
i
j
k
l
m
n
o
p
q
r
s
t
u
v
w
x
y
z

**storey, story**

*Storey* means 'a level in a building'.
> A bungalow is a one-**storey** house. A skyscraper has many **storeys**.

*Story* means 'a tale; a narrative'. A story can be fiction or nonfiction.
> The storyteller told a funny **story**.
> I read the **story** of her life.

**tail, tale**

*Tail* means 'the long, thin, moving rear part of an animal's body'.
> The spider monkey uses its **tail** to grip branches. The horse uses its **tail** to swish flies.

*Tale* means 'a story'.
> Let me tell you the **tale** of the Three Little Pigs.

**their, there, they're**

*Their* is a pronoun that means 'something belongs to *them*'.
> The students opened **their** books and picked up **their** pens.

*There* tells where something is. It means 'in that place'.
> My books are **there** on my desk.

*There* is also used to introduce a sentence.
> **There** is an error in your writing.

*They're* is a shortened form of the words *they are*.
> **They're** members of our team.

**them, those**

*Them* is a pronoun. It takes the place of the word or phrase for people or things that have already been mentioned. In this example, *them* takes the place of *the two dogs*.
> The two dogs were hungry, so Maria fed **them** some dry food.

*Those* is a word that points to a word or phrase for people or things. In this example, *those* points to the words *two dogs*.
> Maria fed **those** two dogs when they were hungry.

**Beware!** It is incorrect to write:
> ✗ Maria fed **them** two dogs some dry food.
> ✗ **Them** two dogs were hungry.

In each of these sentences, the word *those* should be used to point to the phrase *two dogs*.

**tire, tyre**

*Tire* means 'to become sleepy or weary'.
> The runner began to **tire** at the end of the long race.

A *tyre* is the rubber lining on the outside of a wheel.
> His bicycle had a flat **tyre**.

**to, too, two**

*To* is a preposition. It can mean 'towards'.
> The child ran **to** her parents.

*To* can be used as part of a verb.
> He didn't know whether **to run** or **to hide** from the bull.

(*See next page.*→)

76

*Too* has several meanings. It can mean 'extremely'.

> The soup was **too** hot.

*Too* can mean 'more than' or 'beyond'.

> The cookie jar was **too** high for the child to reach.

*Two* means the number 2.

> It takes at least **two** players to play tennis.

## toe, tow

A *toe* is one of the digits on a person's foot.

> He broke his **toe** on a rock.

*Tow* means 'to pull or drag something by a rope or chain'.

> A truck had to **tow** the old car.

## vain, vein

*Vain* means 'being too proud of yourself'.

> He spent so long looking at himself in a mirror that everyone thought he was **vain**.

*Vein* means 'one of the long tubes inside your body that carries blood to your heart'.

> The doctor took a blood sample from a **vein** in my arm.

## waist, waste

*Waist* means 'the part of your body just above your hips'.

> The belt went around my **waist**.

*Waste* can mean 'to not make good use of something'.

> Many people **waste** water.

(*See next column.*→)

*Waste* can mean 'something that has been dumped'.

> Some **waste** from homes and businesses can be recycled.

## wait, weight

*Wait* means 'to stay in one place'.

> I had to **wait** in line at the shop.

*Weight* means 'how heavy something is'.

> The **weight** of the potatoes was too great for the bag, and it burst.

## way, weigh

*Way* can mean 'a direction or path to get somewhere'.

> The car went the wrong **way**.

*Way* can also mean 'a method of doing something'.

> The inventor found a better **way** to wash dishes.

*Weigh* means 'to measure how heavy something is'.

> When cooking something, you should **weigh** the ingredients.

## weak, week

*Weak* means 'not strong'.

> I am **weak** in mathematics.
> The flu made her feel **weak**.

A *week* is seven days.

> I read a book every **week**.

a
b
c
d
e
f
g
h
i
j
k
l
m
n
o
p
q
r
s
t
u
v
w
x
y
z

**weather, whether**

*Weather* means 'the way the wind, clouds, rain and snow behave'.

> The **weather** report helps you to decide what clothes to wear.

*Whether* is a word you can use to introduce choices.

> I don't know **whether** to have a chocolate or a lemon ice cream.

**we'll, wheel**

*We'll* is the shortened form of the words *we will* or *we shall*.

> If it rains, **we'll** take umbrellas.

A *wheel* is a round ring or disk used to let machines or parts move.

> Most cars have four **wheels**.
> Some cycles have one **wheel**.

**were, where**

*Were* is a past-tense form of the verb *to be*. It rhymes with *fur*.

> There **were** so many cars, we could not cross the road.

*Where* means 'in what place'. It rhymes with *air*.

> I don't know **where** they are.
> **Where** did you look?

**what, which**

Both of these words can be used to ask a question.

> **What** is the time?

> **Which** way did they go?

*Which* can take the place of words for people or things that have already been mentioned in a sentence.

> *(See next column.➔)*

My uncle gave me a book. I have read the book twice.

> My uncle gave me a <u>book</u>, **which** I have read twice.

*Which* takes the place of the word *book*. We never use the word *what* in this way.

> ✗ My uncle gave me a book, **what** I have read twice.

**which, witch**

*Which* is a word used to begin a question or connect ideas in a sentence.

> **Which** way did they go?

> They went up the hill, **which** was the wrong way!

*Witch* means 'a person who is supposed to have magical powers'.

> There are many fantasy stories with **witch** characters. The magical powers of a **witch** character let the author create exciting events in the story.

**would've, would of**

See **confusing words**: could've, could of.

**your, you're**

*Your* is another form of the word *you*. It means 'something belongs to you'.

> **Your** dog just chased my cat.

*You're* is the shortened form of the words *you are*.

> Tell me when **you're** ready to go.
> Surely **you're** joking!

# conjunctions

Conjunctions are words that link words and join ideas within a sentence. Here are some examples of conjunctions:

*and*, *but*, *if*, *so*, *or*, *that*, *because*, *when*

Most parrots eat seeds **and** fruit.
In this sentence, the conjunction *and* links the words *seeds* and *fruit*. Without the word *and* the author would have written two sentences. This is clumsy writing.
Most parrots eat seeds. Most parrots eat fruit.

You can use conjunctions to join sentences.
I like parrots. They have beautiful colours.
I like parrots **because** they have beautiful colours.
In this example, the conjunction *because* joined the two sentences. It helps you to understand *why* the person likes parrots.

Conjunctions help you to make your writing flow. Without conjunctions your writing might sound jerky because the sentences are too short. Here is an example without conjunctions:

I like parrots. They have beautiful colours. They have interesting personalities. Sometimes they are a problem. They eat the fruit on my trees. That is OK. I don't mind sharing my fruit.

Here is the same writing with conjunctions:

I like parrots **because** they have beautiful colours **and** interesting personalities. Sometimes they are a problem though **when** they eat the fruit on my trees, **but** that is OK. I don't mind sharing my fruit.

# connectives

Connectives are words or phrases that link ideas within a text. They give the reader a signal about what is happening in the text.

In this example, the connectives are in bold type.

> **At first**, Olivia thought she could eat chocolates for the rest of her life. She began nibbling the big bag of chocolates she got for her birthday. **After a while**, they all tasted the same and she didn't feel so excited about them any more. **In the end**, she felt that she could not face another chocolate for the rest of her life.

The connectives *at first*, *after a while* and *in the end* tell you about the order that things are happening in time. They link the different parts of the text and help you to know where you are in the story.

# consonance

Consonance is the repetition of a consonant sound within words. Authors and poets do this as part of their writing style.

In this example, the /s/ sound is repeated to make you think of a snake.

> **S**ilently the **s**nake **s**lithered pa**s**t the tent while the camper**s** were a**s**leep.

Notice how the /s/ sound can be at the beginning, at the end or in the middle of a word.

For more information, look up **consonants** and **descriptive writing**.

# consonants

There are 21 consonant letters in the alphabet. They are:

**b c d f g h j k l m n p q r s t v w x y z**

The only letters that are not consonants are:

**a e i o u**

These five letters are called *vowels*.

Some consonant letters can have different sounds.
- In the word **cat**, the letter *c* has a /k/ sound as in *kiss*.
- In the word **cell**, the letter *c* has a /s/ sound as in *send*.

The letter *y* sometimes has a consonant sound and sometimes it has a vowel sound.
- In the word **yes**, the letter *y* has a consonant sound.
- In the words **sky** and **mystery**, the *y* has three different vowel sounds.

For more information, see vowels.

# contractions

A contraction is a shortened word or phrase.

Phrases become contractions when letters are left out of words and the phrase becomes one word. An apostrophe shows where letters have been left out.

> **I'll** is a contraction of the phrase **I will**.
> **You're** is a contraction of the phrase **you are**.

Contractions are often used in personal letters, diaries and other types of informal writing.

In stories, when characters are speaking, contractions make the speech sound more natural.

> "I think **I've** broken my arm," cried Mark.
> "**I'll** help you get home," said Jessica.
> "I **can't** move my arm. **It's** too sore," Mark moaned.

If you want to find out more about how to use contractions, see apostrophe (').

81

# correspondence

Correspondence is another word for 'letter writing'. To find out about this, see letter writing.

# could, should, would

*Could* is a form of the verb *can*. It means 'to be able to'.
They **could** win the game if they really tried.

*Should* is a form of the verb *shall*. It means 'ought to'.
We **should** eat vegetables for good health.

*Would* is a form of the verb *will*.
We **would** be lost without the map.

**could've** See **confusing words**: could've, could of.

**could of** See **confusing words**: could've, could of.

**couple** See **confusing words**: couple, few, several.

# couplet

A couplet is a pair of lines in a poem. If the pair of lines rhymes, it is called a *rhyming couplet*.

> When my dog wags his fluffly **tail**,
> It flicks the fleas off without **fail**.

Notice that the lines in the couplet have the same number of beats. The lines in couplets are usually similar in length.

You can add other couplets to make a longer poem.

> When my dog wags his fluffly **tail**,
> It flicks the fleas off without **fail**.
> When other dogs walk past near**by**,
> They start to scratch; I wonder **why**!

**creak** See **confusing words**: creak, creek.

**creek** See **confusing words**: creak, creek.

**currant** See **confusing words**: currant, current.

**current** See **confusing words**: currant, current.

**curtain** See **confusing words**: certain, curtain.

**cymbals** See confusing words: cymbals, symbols.

**dairy** See **confusing words**: dairy, diary.

# dash (—)

The dash is a punctuation mark that is used to separate parts of a sentence. The dashes act a bit like brackets.

The blue whale — **the largest animal of all time** — is found in all the oceans.

In this sentence, the writer used the dashes to add extra information about the blue whale. The dashes separate the extra information from the main sentence.

If you read the sentence without the information between the dashes, the sentence still makes sense.

Dashes can be used to add information at the end of a sentence. Writers sometimes do this to make their sentence sound more exciting.

The lion walked up to the man — **what would it do?**

# dates

When you write the date, you usually include the day, the month and the year. There are different ways to do this. You can use words or numerals.

**Words**

Words are normally used when you write the date within a paragraph or sentence and you are talking about a day and a month only.

My birthday is on the **first of May**.

**Words and numerals**

Words and numerals can be used together when you write the day, the month and the year. Sometimes the words are abbreviated.

He was born on **1st May 2001**.
The party will be held on **16 September 2008**.
A tsunami caused a disaster on **26 Dec 2004**.

**Numerals**

You can write the date using just numerals. The first numeral is for the day, the second for the month and the last numeral is for the year. They are separated by full stops or slashes.

**1.5.2001** (means 1st May 2001)
**16/9/08** (means 16 September 2008)

If you write or read dates in numerals, remember that in the USA they put the month first and the day second. So 1.5.2001 means January the 5th, 2001.

**dear** See **confusing words**: dear, deer.

**deer** See **confusing words**: dear, deer.

# definite/indefinite articles

The words *a*, *an* and *the* are called *articles*. They point to other words and phrases.

The word *the* is called the *definite article*. It is used when you mean a particular thing.

**The** dog barked at **the** intruder.

This sentence talks about a particular dog and a particular intruder, as if they are being pointed out.

The words *a* and *an* are called the *indefinite articles*. You use these words when you are talking about something in general.

**A** dog barked at **the** intruder.

In this sentence, a particular intruder is pointed at, but it could be any dog.

**A** dog barked at **an** intruder.

In this sentence it could be any dog and any intruder. The words *a* and *an* do not point to particular things. That is why they are called the *indefinite* articles.

If you want to know more about this topic, look up a, an, a, the and articles.

# descriptive writing

In descriptive writing, you use words to build a picture of something or someone you want the reader to see and understand. Like an artist, a writer can build a picture of a person or a scene, but using words instead of paint.

Here is a description of a character for a story.

> Into the class came Raymond, as if he owned the place — hands on hips, a loud voice and a confident smile like a coach commanding a football team. Anyone else who wore odd-coloured socks, short pants, a big bow tie and a magician's hat would be laughed at; but no one laughed at Raymond. Ray was cool and trendy — he did what others would like to do but felt afraid of making a fool of themselves. He was a ray of sunshine.

**Notes on style:**

- **Personality** The writer uses *adjectives* to describe Raymond's personality (*confident, loud, cool, trendy*).
- **Appearance** The writer describes Raymond's appearance (unusual clothes).
- **Behaviour** The writer describes Raymond's behaviour (*hands on hips, loud voice*) so you know how he acts with other people.
- **Imagery** The writer uses a *simile* (*like a coach commanding a football team*) and a metaphor (*He was a ray of sunshine.*) to compare Ray to things that might be familiar to you. This is called *imagery*.
- **Sounds** The writer uses the sounds of words in an *alliteration* (**c**onfident smile like a **c**oach **c**ommanding). This makes the words memorable.

To find out more about these methods, see adjectives, alliteration, metaphor and simile.

**desert** See **confusing words**: desert, dessert.

**dessert** See **confusing words**: desert, dessert.

**dew** See **confusing words**: dew, due.

# dialect

A dialect is the special way groups of people in particular places speak a language. For example, people in the USA, England, South Africa, Singapore, Australia and New Zealand might all speak English, but sometimes they might not understand each other because they speak different dialects.

Dialects can be different for several reasons:

- **Accent** (the sounds of the words when people speak)
- **Vocabulary** (the different words people use to mean the same thing)
- **Grammar** (the different ways words are used to make sentences)

Here is what a sentence might sound like if a person from the USA and a person from Australia were speaking:

**(USA)**
Chuck wore his flip flops Monday through Sunday during his vacation in the fall.

**(Australia)**
Charlie wore his thongs from Monday to Sunday during his holiday in autumn.

These sentences mean the same thing, but the words and grammar are different. The sounds of the words would also be different if you heard people say them.

*Dialect* is different from *dialogue*. Dialogue is words characters say to each other. Dialect is the way the characters say and use the words.

There are different dialects within any country. People in Scotland have a different dialect from people in London. People in New York sound different from people in Texas. People in Sydney sound different from people in Alice Springs.

# dialogue

Dialogue is words people say when they speak to each other. Writers often use dialogue in stories; it makes their characters come to life. The way a character speaks can help readers to understand that character better. It also adds a feeling of action to a story.

In this example we can see that the Little Pigs are funny and the Big Bad Wolf is a cunning bully.

---

**"Little pigs, little pigs, please open your door and let me in,"** said the Big Bad Wolf politely.
**"No, we don't want to buy anything,"** chuckled the First Little Pig.
**"Open the door or by the hair on my chinny-chin-chin, I'll huff and I'll puff and I'll blow your house in,"** shouted the Wolf.
**"Oh, my! He's full of wind,"** laughed the Second Little Pig.

---

**Notes on style:**
- Each sentence has two parts: what the characters say, and words that tell you who is speaking.
- Speech marks or quotation marks (" ") surround the words the characters say.

This dialogue can be written as a play script. Then it can be acted as a play. Here is what it would look like.

---

Big Bad Wolf: (*Politely*) **Little pigs, little pigs, please open your door and let me in.**
1st Little Pig: (*Chuckling*) **No, we don't want to buy anything.**
Big Bad Wolf: (*Shouting*) **Open the door or by the hair on my chinny-chin-chin, I'll huff and I'll puff and I'll blow your house in.**
2nd Little Pig: (*Laughing*) **Oh, my! He's full of wind.**

---

**Notes on style:**
- The name of the character speaking is at the beginning of each part of the dialogue.
- Words in brackets (verbs and adverbs) show how the character would speak.

The dialogue between the Little Pigs and the Big Bad Wolf could also be written in speech bubbles (callouts or speech balloons).

Speech bubbles are used in comic strips, cartoons and posters. The pictures tell the reader how the character acts and what the character is like; the speech shows what the character is saying.

All these ways of writing dialogue are called *direct speech*.

To find out more about dialogue, see **direct speech** and **indirect speech**. You will also find more ideas under **humour** and **slang**.

# diary

A diary is writing to record personal experiences and feelings. It is private, usually written just for the author and not to be read by others. A diary is a recount.

Diaries help us to learn about history and how people lived in the past. Famous diaries include *The Diary of Anne Frank* (written by a Jewish girl whose family hid from the Germans in Holland during World War II), and *The Diary of Samuel Pepys* (a man who wrote about the Great Plague, the Great Fire of London and daily life in the 1600s).

Personal diaries are usually a record of true events; they are nonfiction. The diary is also used by fiction writers as a way to tell a story. The writer invents a character and tells the story through that character's diary. This is what a diary might look like:

---

Saturday, April 4
Today I tried to plant my own little vegetable garden. Disaster! The first thing I did was push a pitch fork into the ground. I created an instant fountain as the spikes made two big holes in our automatic watering system pipe. I felt silly. Maybe I'm not cut out to be a gardener. But that's OK. Tomorrow I'll try painting.

---

**Notes on style:**

- It is written from the point of view of the writer. The personal pronouns *I*, *me*, *my*, *mine* are used.
- Diaries are often about the past. Verbs in the past tense (*tried*, *did*, *created*) are used.
- The writer often records personal thoughts or feelings (*I felt silly*).
- The writing is often informal because it is private. Contractions (*I'm*, *that's*, *I'll*) are used.

For more information about this type of writing, see **journal** and **recount**.

**diary** See **confusing words**: dairy, diary.

**die** See **confusing words**: die, dye.

# direct speech

Direct speech is the words spoken by someone. The author writes the words exactly as someone says them.

Direct speech is usually surrounded by quotation marks.

**"I can't find my pen,"** said Danielle.

**"Have you looked in your pocket?"** asked David.
The quotation marks show you the words that Danielle and David actually said.

Danielle said **that she couldn't find her pen**.

David asked **her if she had looked in her pocket**.
In this example, the writer tells you about what Danielle and David said but does not use the words exactly as they said them. This is called *indirect speech* or *reported speech*.

To find other ways to write direct speech, look up dialogue and speech.

# discussion

A discussion text is nonfiction writing that gives you more than one point of view. It shows you different ways of thinking about a topic.

A discussion text usually has:
- an **introduction**
- **information** (opinions) from two or more people
- a **conclusion** or summary

In the following example, two people give opinions on a topic.

(Turn the page to see the example of discussion. →)

a
b
c
**d**
e
f
g
h
i
j
k
l
m
n
o
p
q
r
s
t
u
v
w
x
y
z

### THE BEST LIFE: CITY OR COUNTRY?

Is it better to live in a city or in the country? Michael and Melanie tell you what they think.

**Michael's opinion**

I've lived in the country all my life, so I know that it is the best place to live. The air is fresh, not like a city. So the country is a healthier environment. You have plenty of space and there are no traffic jams.

**Melanie's opinion**

I've always lived in the city. There is so much to do in a city. I can go to museums, the theatre, theme parks and great places to eat. I think I would get bored living in the country.

**Summary**

Michael says the country is healthier and more spacious. Melanie says the city has more interesting things to do. However, both Michael and Melanie have lived in only one place. What would someone who has lived in both the country and the city say?

**Introduction**

The writer asks a question so you know what the discussion will be about. The introduction also tells you who is going to give an opinion on the topic.

**Information**

Both Michael and Melanie give their information (opinions) and reasons for their opinions.

**Summary**

The writer sums up the different viewpoints by mentioning the main points made by Michael and Melanie. The last sentence comments on the information and speakers.

To find more information and examples, see argument.

**doe** See confusing words: doe, dough.

**dot points** See bullet points (•).

# double negative

A negative is a word that gives a sentence the meaning of 'no' or 'not'. When a writer uses two negatives in a sentence, it is called a *double negative.*

Double negatives undo the meaning of 'no' or 'not' in a sentence. Careful writers usually make sure that they do not use double negatives.

There were **no** cookies in the jar.
The word *no* gives this sentence a negative meaning.

There **weren't no** cookies in the jar.
The word *weren't* (*were not*) adds another negative to the sentence. This makes it a double negative (*weren't no*). Does this mean there really were some cookies?

Writers sometimes overuse negatives as a way of emphasising something. Here is an example of this.

> **Speak up, Bobby!**
> Bobby said, "I **don't** eat **no** spinach,
> And I sure **don't** eat **no** eggs."
> If Bobby **don't** eat **no** cabbage,
> He **won't** get **no** meat on his legs.
> Bobby **won't never** stay healthy,
> He'll get smaller and smaller each day,
> Till he **won't** be **hardly nothing**,
> And we'll **not never hardly** hear him s-a-a-a-a-a-y...
> "I **don't** eat no spinach..."
> SPEAK UP BOY! WE **CAN'T HARDLY** HEAR **NOTHING**!

## Notes on style:

- The words *can't*, *don't*, *no*, *won't*, *never*, *not*, *nothing* and *hardly* are all negative words.
- The author uses so many negatives that they make the meaning purposely ridiculous. There is a double negative in almost every line and sometimes *three* negatives.

(By the way, the last line means that the speaker cannot hear anything.)

If you want to find out more, see **negatives**.

**dough** See **confusing words**: doe, dough.

# drafting

Drafting is an important step in the writing process. It is when authors first put their ideas together as writing. They can do this either on paper or on a computer.

The ideas for your first draft come from brainstorming with others. You can also read other books to research information and make notes. These notes are then organised into an order that makes sense. It can be a good idea to use headings when you do this.

When you write your draft, do not worry about whether your spelling is correct or whether you should begin a new paragraph. Just write your ideas in sentences. Correct the spelling, the sentences and the paragraphs when you begin the next step — revising.

To find out more about the editing process, see editing and revising. You could also look up writing process to find out about all the steps in writing. You'll find an example of an author's ideas, draft and revised writing.

# drama

A *drama* is a story played out by actors on stage, television, film, video, radio, CD, DVD or any other way actors can reach an audience.

The actors become the characters in the story. They tell the story by speaking to each other (dialogue). The dialogue is usually written in a play script. The script also tells the actors how to show feelings and how to move on stage.

To find out more about how to write drama, see dialogue and play script.

**draw** See **confusing words**: draw, drawer.

**drawer** See **confusing words**: draw, drawer.

**due** See **confusing words**: dew, due.

**dye** See **confusing words**: die, dye.

94

# -e

The letter *e* at the end of many words is usually not sounded. However, often when *e* comes after a consonant at the end of a word, it gives a vowel in front of the consonant a long sound.

h**o**p / h**o**pe

In this example, the letter *o* has a short sound in the word *hop* (to rhyme with *stop*). In *hope*, the letter *o* has a long sound (to rhyme with *rope*). Here are some other examples:

*mad / made*, *them / theme*, *strip / stripe*, *cut / cute*

Some words ending in the letter *e* do not obey this rule. Here are some examples:

*give*, *have*, *love*, *dove*, *prince*, *rinse*, *fence*, *badge*

# editing

Editing is an important step in the writing process. At this stage, the draft writing is revised and improved to make it ready for publication.

## Revising

In the first part of editing, the writer reads the first draft and fixes the obvious problems.

HINT: It is a good idea to put your draft away for a while before you read and revise it. It is easier to see problems in your writing that way.

The main problems to look for at this stage are:

• ideas that do not belong to your topic
• information that is wrong
• paragraphs that are in the wrong order
• sentences that do not make sense or are hard to understand

(Turn the page for more about editing. →)

### Editing

After revising their draft, it is hard for most professional writers to edit their own writing — they need an editor to help them. Other people can find it easier to see the problems in your writing. It is a good idea to swap your revised draft with someone else. You could edit each other's work.

The main problems an editor first looks for are:

- information or events that are in the wrong order
- characters, settings and events that do not make sense or do not belong together in a story
- information that is wrong or does not make sense
- sentences that do not make sense or are unclear

### Proofreading

After fixing the problems your editor found, the last step is to proofread your writing and look for errors in spelling, punctuation and capital letters.

If you want to know more, see **writing process**.

**effect** See **confusing words**: affect, effect.

**ei, ie** Go to **spelling** to find information about words spelled with these letters.

**either** See **confusing words**: either, neither.

# ellipsis points (...)

Ellipsis points are a punctuation mark that shows something has been left out in a sentence or that a speaker has been cut off.

> **Tom**: (Answers the telephone) Hello.
> **Voice**: Hello. I'm selling pet food. Do you have a**...**

The ellipsis points show that the voice on the telephone did not finish the sentence, possibly because Tom hung up the phone.

# email

The word *email* is short for *electronic mail*. People write letters or notes on a computer and send them through the Internet as email.

Email has become the most popular way for people to write letters or messages to each other because it is so quick and so cheap.

You can attach photographs, charts, music, voice and video to an email. Here is what an email might look like.

**To**: emma@xxxyzzz.com
**Cc**:
**Subject**: Weekend sleep over

Hi Emma
My parents have said it is OK for me to have someone sleep over on the weekend. Are you free? By the way, I've attached a photo of us at the party last week. You look great. I look like a clown!
See ya. :-)
Rosa

Party pair.jpg

**Notes on style:**
- The email address of the receiver is in the 'To' box.
- The topic of the email is written in the 'Subject' box.
- The writing is informal because it is to a friend. (Rosa uses the words *Hi* and *See ya*. She also uses a 'smile' sign *:-)*.)
- A photo is attached at the end of the email.

If you want to know more about writing letters, see letter writing. You can find more examples of formal and informal language at formal/informal writing.

**ewe** See **confusing words**: ewe, yew, you.

**except** See **confusing words**: accept, except.

97

# exclamation mark (!)

The *exclamation mark* is a punctuation mark used at the end of a sentence. Writers use it to show strong feelings such as happiness, surprise, disgust or amazement.

> That dog stinks! Give it a bath!
> Call the fire department, quickly!

Often, the exclamation mark is used after a word or phrase.

> Ah! Help!
> Absolutely fantastic!

Read these two lines. How does the exclamation mark change the way you read the second sentence?

> I don't believe it.
> I don't believe it!

Exclamation marks are often used with interjections.

> **Ooh! Ah! Ouch!** That hurts.

For more about words like this, see interjections.

# exclamations

Exclamations are words, phrases or sentences that express strong feelings such as fear, surprise, excitement or happiness. They usually end with an exclamation mark.

> The circus was really amazing!
> Send that dog outside, now!
> Silence, please!

# explanation

An *explanation text* is nonfiction writing that explains how something works or happens. For example, it might explain how machines work or why storms happen.

There are two main parts to an explanation:

- The **introduction** to the topic
- The **details** of the explanation — beginning with what happens first and ending with what happens last

An explanation text often has diagrams that tell you the names of things that are part of the explanation. These diagrams can also have arrows to show how and where these parts move.

(Turn the page to see an example of an explanation text about how clouds are formed.→)

### HOW CLOUDS FORM

**Introduction**

You can often see clouds in the sky, but where do they come from? This text tells you.

**Water Enters the Air**

Water in places such as seas, lakes, rivers and ponds is always turning into a gas called *water vapour*. This is helped by the sun and the wind. Water vapour is invisible as it enters the air, so you cannot see it.

**Warm Air Rises**

If the water vapour is in warm air, it rises. You can see this with a hot-air balloon. The warm air in the balloon rises and takes the balloon with it. In nature, warm air rises and so the water vapour rises with it.

**Cool Air**

Air that is high in the sky is usually cooler than air near the ground. The air gets very cold where planes fly. As the warm air rises, it too gradually gets cooler, which causes the water vapour to turn from a gas into very small droplets of water. This is like mist. When the water vapour does this, you begin to see it as clouds.

**Notes on style**

This explanation text has:

- The introduction, telling you what the topic is about
- Verbs in the present tense (*is helped*, *enters*, *rises*)
- Words that tell the order things happen (*as*, *when*)
- Words that link causes to things that happen (*so*, *which causes*)
- A labelled diagram to explain movement and change

# exposition

In an *exposition* (or *expository writing*) the writer gives evidence to prove a point of view or an idea. Expository writing is a type of argument.

There are three main parts to an exposition:

1. A **description** of a point of view about a topic
2. **Arguments and evidence** to prove the point of view
3. A **summary** to remind the reader of the topic, the point of view and the evidence that proves it

Here is an example of an exposition.

> **THE INTER-SCHOOL SWIMMING CARNIVAL**
> Pinbrook and Angelsea Schools will be competing in a swimming carnival one month from today. I believe that our school, Pinbrook, will not win the swimming carnival this year.
>
> In the first place, the Angelsea swimming team does two hours training each morning, seven days a week, while the Pinbrook team does only one hour on five days a week. The Angelsea team is fitter.
>
> Secondly, Pinbrook's fastest swimmer, Jose Elviro, moved to another school not long ago. This made our team weaker. Angelsea has lost none of its top swimmers.
>
> Because of the facts about fitness and key team members, in my opinion, Angelsea will win the Inter-school Swimming Carnival.

**Notes on style:**

- Use verbs like *believe* and *think* for giving an opinion.
- Use words like *in the first place* and *secondly* to list arguments and evidence in a clear order.
- Use words like *because* and *while* to link evidence to each opinion.

For more information, see argument.

**ewe** See **confusing words**: ewe, yew, you.

# fable

A fable is a very short story that has a moral or a lesson. Fables usually have only two characters — often animals that act like humans. The moral is usually written at the end of the story.

Here is an example of a simple traditional fable.

---

### The Two Goats

Two goats both tried to cross a deep valley by walking over a log bridge. However, they were going in opposite ways and came head to head in the middle of the log.

"I got here first," said one goat, "so *you* have to give way to *me*."

"I think I got here before you," said the other goat. "*You* give way."

Neither goat would give way. They charged each other and butted heads. Then, together they slipped and fell into the valley below.

*Fighting does not solve problems.*

---

**Notes on style:**
- There are just two characters (animals)
- Characters and problem are told in the first paragraph
- Only one event happens: the characters fight and fall
- The characters speak to each other (dialogue)
- The moral at the end tells you the theme — the main idea of the story. (It does not mention the characters.)
- The story is in the past tense (*tried*, *were going*, *came*), but the moral is in the present tense (*does not solve*)

For other kinds of stories that teach a lesson, see allegory, cautionary tale and parable.

**fair** See **confusing words**: fair, fare.

102

# fairytale

A fairytale is a story in which magic is used to cause or solve the problems the characters meet. A fairytale does not necessarily have fairies, but it will have some form of fantasy characters such as beasts, dragons, dwarfs, elves, fairy godmothers, goblins, giants, ogres, witches and wizards.

Many of the best known fairytales are very old. Here is a famous fairytale by Charles Perrault.

### Sleeping Beauty (The Briar Rose)

ONCE UPON a time, a king and a queen were unhappy because they had no child. One day, the queen did a kind deed and saved a poor animal in trouble. The animal told the queen that she would have her wish for a child come true. Just as she was promised, the queen gave birth to a beautiful baby girl.

A huge party was held to celebrate the birth of the baby princess and all in the land were invited, including the twelve fairies. There was a thirteenth fairy, but no one liked her because she was always nasty.

At the party, the good fairies wished wonderful things for the baby. As the eleventh fairy gave her blessing, the nasty fairy arrived.

"How dare you not invite *me*!' she screeched. "I cast a curse that when the princess is fifteen, she will prick her finger on a spindle and die!" At that moment, the evil fairy just vanished.

The king and queen were horrified about the curse, but the twelfth fairy stepped forward.

"Do not worry," she said. "I have not yet given the princess my good wishes. I cannot undo the evil spell, but I promise you the princess will not die. She will fall into a deep sleep for one hundred years. Then a prince will find her and awaken her with a kiss."

To protect their daughter, the king ordered that every spindle in the land be burned. The princess grew into a beautiful young girl. Then, just after her fifteenth birthday she was exploring an empty part of the castle when she found a strange old woman making thread on a spinning wheel.

(Turn the page to find out what happens. →)

Having not seen a spinning wheel before, the princess picked up the spindle and tried to spin some wool, but she pricked her finger. The curse began and she fell to the floor. Just then the twelfth fairy entered the castle and waved her wand. Everyone in the castle fell asleep. Tall, prickly, briar rose bushes surrounded the castle walls.

And so for ninety-nine years, the princess slept and no one could reach the castle. The princess became known as Briar Rose, and eventually her story reached the ears of a prince in a faraway land. He travelled for many months to find this princess. Finally he found the famous castle, one hundred years after the curse was cast.

As the prince approached the castle, the briar roses wilted away, but sprang up again behind him so others could not follow. The prince walked past all the sleeping guards and servants and searched until he found the princess lying peacefully on the floor. She was still beautiful — so beautiful that the prince kneeled and kissed her.

The princess opened her eyes and gazed at the prince. As they walked through the castle, all the other palace people also awoke from their sleep and carried on working as if nothing had happened.

The prince and princess grew to love each other, and so they married. Once again the king and queen gave a big party to celebrate and everyone lived happily ever after.

**Notes on style:**
- The setting is a fantasy land far away and long ago (*Once upon a time*).
- Main good and evil characters have magical powers.
- The story has several stages and events.
- The verbs are in the past tense (*did*, *saved*, *told*).
- The hero (*a prince*) is brave and adventurous.
- The characters finish where they began (*people also awoke from their sleep and carried on as if nothing had happened*).
- Good wins over evil, and the story ends well (*everyone lived happily ever after*).

Other old fairytales include *Rapunzel, Hansel and Gretel, Snow White and the Seven Dwarfs, Jack and the Beanstalk, Rumpelstiltskin* and *Cinderella*.

# fantasy

Fantasy writing is about imaginary worlds where anything can happen, and imaginary characters who can do anything. The author takes the reader into a kind of dream world which might be in the past, the present or the future.

In a fantasy story:
- The characters might be animals, monsters, imaginary creatures, rocks, trees or humans
- The story might happen in outer space, underground or in an imaginary world invented by the writer
- Characters might have magical powers
- Animals might be able to talk and think like humans

Here are some well-known fantasy stories:
*Peter Pan* by J M Barrie
*The Wind in the Willows* by Kenneth Grahame
*Alice's Adventures in Wonderland* by Lewis Carroll
*The Hobbit* by J R R Tolkein
*The Magic Pudding* by Norman Lindsay
*The Legend of Sleepy Hollow* by Washington Irving
*The Little Mermaid* by Hans Christian Andersen
*The Adventures of Pinocchio* by Carlo Collodi
*Harry Potter* (series) by J K Rowling

**fare** See **confusing words**: fair, fare.

**farther** See **confusing words**: farther, father and farther, further.

**fate** See **confusing words**: fate, fete.

**father** See **confusing words**: farther, father.

**fete** See **confusing words**: fate, fete.

**few** See **confusing words**: couple, few, several.

**fewer** See **confusing words**: fewer, less.

# fiction

*Fiction* is writing that is created from the writer's imagination. The characters, the settings and what happens in the stories and poems are invented by the author.

There are many ways to write fiction. It might be a novel, a poem or a play.

If you want to know more about particular kinds of fiction, you can find them in this *Junior Writers Guide* under these headings:

*adventure stories, allegory, anecdote, animal stories, ballad, cautionary tale, drama, fable, fairy-tale, fantasy, folktale, legend, myth, narrative, novel, parable, parody, plays, poetry, saga, short stories*

To find out about writing that is not fiction, look up nonfiction.

**film script** See screenplay.

**fir** See **confusing words**: fir, fur.

**flaw** See **confusing words**: flaw, floor.

**flea** See **confusing words**: flea, flee.

**flee** See **confusing words**: flea, flee.

**flew** See **confusing words**: flew, flu, flue.

**floor** See **confusing words**: flaw, floor.

**flour** See **confusing words**: flour, flower.

**flower** See **confusing words**: flour, flower.

**flu** See **confusing words**: flew, flu, flue.

**flue** See **confusing words**: flew, flu, flue.

# folktale

A folktale is a traditional story that storytellers have passed on for hundreds of years. Every culture has its own collection of folktales. *Folk* means 'people'. So folktales are stories of the people.

There are different styles of folktales. Here are five examples of different types you might find in a library.

### Fools' tales

These tales have characters who do foolish things that get them into trouble. Here is an example.

> **The Husband, the Wife and the Boat**
>
> A husband and wife lived on an island by themselves. Their boat was their only way of getting to the mainland to buy food. One day they argued over who should row across the water to do the shopping.
>
> "I'm not going because I went last time. It's your turn," said the husband.
>
> "I do all the cooking," said the wife. "I'm not going to do the shopping as well."
>
> They argued all day and became very angry. At last, the husband picked up an axe and cut a big hole in the boat.
>
> "Now," he said, "I don't have to go. The boat would sink."

### Beast tales

These tales have giants, ogres, beasts or monsters as characters. Two examples are:
*Beauty and the Beast*
*Jack and the Beanstalk*

### Trickster tales

These tales are about people who use their wits to solve a problem by tricking another character.

(Turn the page for an example of a trickster tale.→)

## Hedda and the Ogre

Hedda was looking after her goats when a big ogre came out of the forest. She was afraid that he would eat her or her goats. Quickly she asked him a question.

"Ogre, can you squeeze water out of a stone?"

"Of course I can," said the ogre, boasting.

Hedda carefully took an egg out of her pocket and squeezed it. The egg cracked and dripped from her hand. The ogre picked up a stone and squeezed as hard as he could, but nothing came out of it.

"Can you crush a stone to powder?" asked Hedda.

"Of course I can," said the ogre, bragging about his strength.

Hedda took a lump of salt from her pocket and squeezed it. Salt sprinkled to the ground. The ogre went quiet.

"I'll do that tomorrow," he said. "It's late and I need to rest."

Hedda did not trust the ogre. She put some rocks under her rug and hid behind a tree. During the night, the ogre crept up to her rug and threw a big boulder down onto it.

"Ha! Now she won't be any trouble," he said.

"Oh, the bugs are so bad," said Hedda in the dark. "My head feels itchy."

The ogre was amazed. He became frightened of this girl who was stronger than he, so he ran into the night and was not seen again.

Another example is the story of *The Emperor's New Clothes.* Some clever tailors trick a proud emperor into thinking he is wearing the finest cloth in the world, but he is really wearing nothing.

### 'How and Why' tales

These tales explain why something is so. They are also called *legends* or *pourquoi tales* (from the French word *pourquoi* meaning 'why'). Two examples might be:

*How the Zebra Got Its Stripes*
*Where the Milky Way Came From*

**for** See **confusing words**: for, four.

# formal/informal writing

When writers want people to think their message is important, they use formal language. They make sure the writing is correct. Formal writing makes a message sound more proper, polite and serious.

When writers want their message to be personal and casual, they use informal language. They use words that don't sound so official. Informal writing makes a message sound more relaxed.

**Formal letter**

> Mr William White
> 14 Count St
>
> Dear Mr White,
> I am writing to inform you that your dog bit my dog on the leg as we were walking past your property. My dog needed treatment by the veterinarian. I request that you pay the cost of these medical services.
>
> Yours faithfully,
> Ms Susan Green

**Informal letter**

> Hi Billy,
> Just letting you know that as I was walking my dog past your place, your dog jumped out and bit my dog! The vet says he's OK, but I'd appreciate it if you would pay the vet's bill.
> Regards, Susie

**foul** See **confusing words**: foul, fowl.

**four** See **confusing words**: for, four.

**fowl** See **confusing words**: foul, fowl.

# free verse

*Free verse* is poetry that focuses on the meaning of the words and building word pictures. It does not rhyme or have a set pattern or rhythm.

---

**Butterfly**
Like a leaf in the wind,
It flutters by,
Flittering, flapping and falling on flowers;
Sucking, sipping, sampling nectar
From the garden
food mall.

---

In free verse, you need to choose a topic and describe it or tell a tale about it. Although you do not have to worry about rhyme and rhythm, you do need to make sure that your words give the reader a clear picture of the topic.

**Notes on style:**
In the example, the author built a word picture with:
- a **simile** to compare (*Like a leaf in the wind*)
- **alliteration** (*flittering, fluttering, flapping and falling on flowers*)
- **action verbs** (*flutters, flittering, flapping, falling, sucking, sipping, sampling*)
- **metaphor** (*From the garden food mall*)
- **word position** (changing the line beginnings to look like the flittering of a butterfly)

To find out about the methods the author has used, see alliteration, metaphor, simile and verbs.

**-fs, -ves** For information on words like *knife/knives*, see plural.

**fur** See **confusing words**: fir, fur.

**further** See **confusing words**: farther, further.

# full stop (.)

The *full stop* is one of the oldest punctuation marks in English writing. It is used more often than other marks. It is also called a *period.*

### In abbreviations

Full stops are used in some abbreviations to show that the word has been shortened. People are using the full stop less in abbreviations than they used to.

9 **a.m.** We started lessons at school.
The full stops in the abbreviation *a.m.* make sure that you do not think the word is *am*.

### In sentences

The full stop marks the end of a sentence.

The first lesson was reading. I read with a group.

The exclamation mark (!), the question mark (?) and the ellipsis points (...) are also used to end a sentence.

### With numerals

When a full stop is used to mark the units and the tenths in a numeral, it is called a *decimal point*.

They ran for **1.5** hours before stopping to rest.

**fur** See **confusing words**: fir, fur.

**further** See **confusing words**: farther, further.

# genre

*Genre* means 'text type'. It is a name given to the different forms of writing. Writers use different genres, or text types, to suit their reason for writing to an audience. Each genre has its own structure, grammar and style.

To find out more about each genre or text type, see argument, discussion, explanation, narrative, poetry, procedural text, recount, report and review.

# geographical names

The names of particular places in the world begin with a capital letter.

> The tallest mountain in the world is **Mount Everest** in the **Himalayan Mountains** between the countries of **Nepal** and **Tibet**. Of all the oceans, the **Pacific Ocean** is the largest.

Place names have a capital letter even when they are shortened or abbreviated.

> Hilary and Tensing were the first people to successfully climb **Mt** Everest.

# glossary

A glossary is a list that explains technical words. Glossaries are often used in nonfiction texts. They give the meanings of words that are not explained in the text.

A glossary is placed at the end of a book. The words are listed in alphabetical order, like a dictionary.

---

**GLOSSARY**
**eyrie** The nest of an eagle or other bird of prey
**fledgling** A young bird beginning to fly
**honeyeater** A bird that feeds on nectar in flowers
**plume** A large feather
**talon** The hooked claw on a bird of prey

---

**good** See **confusing words**: good, well.

# grammar

Grammar is the way we describe how our language works. It helps writers to know whether their sentences will make sense to readers.

Grammar is a set of rules people use with words, phrases and sentences to make meaning.

Writers and editors use grammar to know how they can change words, phrases and sentences to make their writing clearer.

In grammar, we use words to name parts of speech (*nouns*, *pronouns*, *verbs*, etc). They make it easier to talk about how the language works. You can find out more about this if you look up parts of speech.

# grateful

*Grateful* is sometimes spelled incorrectly as *greatful*. This word does not mean 'great'. It means 'thankful'. The spelling *grate* in this word comes from the Latin word *gratus* meaning 'pleased' or 'thankful'. Your readers will be grateful if you spell it correctly!

**guessed** See **confusing words**: guessed, guest.

**guest** See **confusing words**: guessed, guest.

a
b
c
d
e
f
g
h
i
j
k
l
m
n
o
p
q
r
s
t
u
v
w
x
y
z

**a b c d e f g** 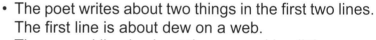 **h** **i j k l m n o p q r s t u v w x y z**

**had've** See **confusing words**: could've, could of.

**had of** See **confusing words**: could've, could of.

# haiku

*Haiku* is a type of Japanese poem. A haiku poem has three lines that do not rhyme. Here is an example:

> **Morning Light**
> Dew on spider's web,
> Sun's rays like little rainbows;
> A chandelier

In haiku, the poet uses very few words to describe an idea or a feeling in a clever way. This makes the poet choose the words carefully.

- The poet writes about two things in the first two lines.
  The first line is about dew on a web.
  The second line is about the sun making little rainbows through the dewdrops.
  These lines build a word picture.
- In the last line, the poet compares sparkling dewdrops on a spider web to a chandelier. The poet is being clever with a pun: a chandelier is a beautiful *light* fitting and the poem is called *Morning Light*.

A haiku is organised in a special way, with three lines.
- It has five syllables in the first line.
- It has seven syllables in the second line.
- It has five syllables in the last line.

**Notes on style:**

To build a word picture, the poet uses:
- a **simile** (*like little rainbows*)
- a **metaphor** (compares the picture to a chandelier)
- **alliteration** (*like little*)
- **sibilance** (the /s/ sound in *Sun's rays*, *rainbows*)

Find more about these methods under alliteration, metaphor, pun, sibilance, simile and syllable.

**hair** See **confusing words**: hair, hare.

**hanged** See **confusing words**: hanged, hung.

**hare** See **confusing words**: hair, hare.

**heal** See **confusing words**: heal, heel, he'll.

**hear** See **confusing words**: hear, here.

**heard** See **confusing words**: heard, herd.

**heel** See **confusing words**: heal, heel, he'll.

**heir** See **confusing words**: air, heir.

**he'll** See **confusing words**: heal, heel, he'll.

**herd** See **confusing words**: heard, herd.

**here** See **confusing words**: hear, here.

# high-frequency words

Although there are over 600,000 words in the English language, some words are used much more often than others. These are called *high-frequency words*. It is important for writers to know how to spell and use these words. Here are fifty of the most used words in English.

*I, up, look, we, like, and, on, at, for, he, is, said, go, you, are, this, going, they, away, play, a, am, cat, to, come, day, the, dog, big, my, mum, no, dad, all, get, in, went, was, of, me, she, see, it, yes, can, about, after, again, an, another*

**him** See **confusing words**: him, hymn.

**hoarse** See **confusing words**: hoarse, horse.

**hole** See **confusing words**: hole, whole.

# homographs

Homographs are words that have the same spelling but different sounds and meanings. They are a type of homonym.

(Turn the page for some examples of homographs. →)

a
b
c
d
e
f
g
**h**
i
j
k
l
m
n
o
p
q
r
s
t
u
v
w
x
y
z

### bow

- (*bow* rhymes with *low*) The musician used a **bow** to play the violin.
- (*bow* rhymes with *now*) I had to **bow** down to get under the wire fence.

### desert

- (pronounced /**dez**-ert/) Camels live in the **desert**.
- (pronounced /dee-**zert**/) They had to **desert** their treehouse in the storm.

### lead

- (*lead* rhymes with *bed*) **Lead** is a heavy metal.
- (*lead* rhymes with *seed*) He took the **lead** in the race.

### minute

- (pronounced /**min**-ut/) She took only a **minute** to climb the stairs.
- (pronounced /my-**nyoot**/) The bug was so **minute** he needed a magnifying glass to see it.

### read

- (*read* rhymes with *seed*) At school you learn to **read**.
- (*read* rhymes with *bed*) He **read** the book last night.

### row

- (*row* rhymes with *go*) The soldiers marched in a **row**.
- (*row* rhymes with *now*) The brothers had a **row** over what to watch on TV.

### sow

- (*sow* rhymes with *go*) The farmer got a new machine to **sow** the wheat.
- (*sow* rhymes with *now*) A **sow** is a female pig.

### tear

- (*tear* rhymes with *hear*) There was a **tear** in his eye.
- (*tear* rhymes with *hair*) There is a **tear** in his pants.

### wind

- (*wind* rhymes with *grinned*) The **wind** blew my kite.
- (*wind* rhymes with *find*) I will **wind** in my fishing line.

### wound

- (*wound* rhymes with *crooned*) The **wound** bled.
- (*wound* rhymes with *round*) She **wound** up the clock.

116

# homonyms

Homonyms are words that have the same sound or spelling but different meanings.

The words **bear** and **bare** sound the same, but they are spelled differently and they have different meanings. Words like this are called *homophones*. They are a type of homonym.

To find out about many other words like this, see confusing words.

The word **wind** can have two different sounds and two different meanings. Words like this are called *homographs*. They are a type of homonym.

To find out more about the different types of homonyms, see homographs and homophones.

To find out how to have fun and make jokes with homonyms, see pun.

# homophones

Homophones are words that have the same sound but different meanings. They are a type of homonym. There are many pairs of homophones, but sometimes there can be three or four words that are homophones. Here are some examples:

> *to, too, two*
> *paw, poor, pore, pour*

Homophones often cause a problem when a writer uses the wrong spelling for the meaning wanted.

For a long list of words that sound the same or look the same, see confusing words.

**horse** See **confusing words**: hoarse, horse.

**hour** See **confusing words**: hour, our.

# humour

Humour is writing in any text type that makes the audience laugh. Different kinds of text can do this. There are also different methods and styles authors use to make people laugh. Here are some of those texts and styles.

### Anecdote

An anecdote is a short story about one event or happening. People often tell funny anecdotes about what happened to them, their family members, friends or pets. An anecdote might begin with words like "A funny thing happened to me the other day when..."

For an example, see anecdote.

### Cartoon

A cartoon is a funny drawing, usually with speech (dialogue) for the character(s) in the drawing. The humour is in the way the characters are drawn and what they say. The speech is written in speech bubbles so you know who is saying the words.

You can use a series of cartoons to tell a short story or joke; this is called a comic strip. Here is an example.

For more about cartoons, see callout and dialogue.

### Comedy

Comedy is a funny story told through acting. This might happen as a play on stage, a television show, a radio play or a film. Comedy is written as a play script so the actors know the words they should say.

For more about comedy, see dialogue and play script.

### Fools' tale

These are short stories with silly characters who do foolish things and get themselves into a hopeless mess.

To find out more about fools' tales, see folktale.

### Joke

A joke is a very short story that has a funny last sentence. This is called the *punchline* because it is the line that makes the reader laugh.

There are many different styles of joke. One of the simplest is the question-and-answer joke.

> On the first day of a new school year, a boy took a ladder to school.
>
> A teacher said, "Why did you bring the ladder to school?"
>
> The boy said, "Because this is a high school!"

### Limerick

Limericks are funny poems with five lines. Their rhyming pattern is A A B B A. They have two long lines, two short lines, then one long line.

> A clever young girl named Greer,
> Could spell any word she could hear,
> In Greek, French and Danish,
> Welsh, Dutch and Spanish,
> Butt Inglish werds trickt hir its klear.

HINTS:
- The first two lines introduce the topic and the person.
- The two short lines give more detail about the topic.
- The last line surprises the reader (in this example by spelling all the words incorrectly).
- This poem is funny because the person can spell words in other languages but not in her own language. This is a joke about spelling in English.

(Turn the page for more about humour.→)

a
b
c
d
e
f
g
h
i
j
k
l
m
n
o
p
q
r
s
t
u
v
w
x
y
z

### Parody

Parody is making fun of something serious or famous. You can make fun of an old story, a popular song or a poem. It is funny when the audience knows the original story or poem and knows the writer is playing with it.

In a parody it is important to write in the same style as the original poem or story so the reader remembers it. Then change some parts so it sounds silly.

> Mary had a little lamb,
> Its fleece was white as snow.
> But it became a big fat sheep,
> So to market it did go!

### Riddle

Riddles are questions that give clues to a tricky answer.

> **Question**: When is an ant as big as a truck?
> **Answer**: When it's an eleph-ant.
>
> **Question**: Where does the elephant keep its clothes?
> **Answer**: In its trunk.

### Tall tale

Tall tales are funny because they brag about or exaggerate what a character can do. The reader knows the character cannot really do all the things in the story. Examples of tall tales and characters are:

*Pecos Bill Rides a Tornado* (USA)
*Baron Münchausen* (Germany)
*Big Ned and the Eggs* (Australia)

### Find out about techniques

There are special techniques writers use to create funny texts. To find out about some techniques, see hyperbole, nonsense, pun, sarcasm and word play.

**hung** See **confusing words**: hanged, hung.

**hymn** See **confusing words**: him, hymn.

# hyperbole

Hyperbole (/hi-**per**-buh-lee/) means 'exaggerating something on purpose'. Writers do this to emphasise a point or to be funny.

> They spoke *at a million words a minute*.
> The suitcase was so heavy, *we got a crane to lift it*.
> The train was so slow *we got off, planted seeds, went to the back of the train and picked the flowers*.

Hyperbole is very useful when you write a comedy, a tall tale, a joke, a limerick, a parody or a review. Look up humour to find out more about these topics.

# hyphen (-)

The hyphen is a small dash that joins or splits words or word parts. It is used mainly to show that some words or word parts should be read as one word.

**Compound words**
Some words are made of other words joined by a hyphen. They are called *compound words* because they are made up of more than one word.

> **twenty-one**, **great-grandfather**, **mother-in-law**

Some words begin as two parts joined with a hyphen (*e-mail*). As they become better known, they often become one word (*email*).

**Word breaks**
Hyphens are used to break a word when it will not fit at the end of a line of text. The word breaks are made between syllables in a word. Each part of a word in a word break should sound as it does in the whole word.

> *X* I could not finish the puzzle because three **jigs-aw** pieces were missing.
> ✓ I could not finish the puzzle because three **jig-saw** pieces were missing.

If you are not sure where to split a word, or whether a word should have a hyphen, check in your dictionary.

# idiom

An idiom is a saying that has a different meaning from what the words seem to mean.

(Idiom) **Keep your nose to the grindstone.**
(Meaning) Work hard.

Here are some other common idioms:
**on thin ice** means 'acting unsafely or at risk'
**caught red-handed** means 'caught in the act'
**a red herring** means 'something misleading'
**stab in the dark** means 'to guess at something'

Idioms are useful when you want to make characters' dialogue in stories sound natural.

"You're **on thin ice** if you try to trick me," said the sheriff.

**Beware!**

Idioms can make your writing hard to understand. They are a problem to people who are learning English, because the words do not mean exactly what they say.

When idioms are used too often, they become *clichés*. They can make your writing sound boring. For more about this, see cliché.

# ie

To find out whether words are spelled with *ei* or *ie*, look up spelling.

# ie (i.e.)

These letters are an abbreviation of a Latin phrase and mean 'that is'. They are always followed by a comma.

# impersonal writing

Impersonal writing sounds as if the writing or the book is speaking to you. It is not written from the writer's point of view.

In the following example, the text says 'this book' is doing the telling. The author also uses the pronoun *it*. This makes the language sound impersonal.

**This book tells you** about penguins. **It** describes where they live and what they eat.

In the example below, the text says that the author is doing the telling. It has the pronoun *I*. This is personal writing. It sounds as if the author is talking to you.

In this book **I tell you** about penguins. **I** describe where they live and what they eat.

Impersonal writing is used a lot in nonfiction. In the following example, the pronouns *it* and *its* make the writing sound factual and scientific.

The penguin is a bird. **It** has very small wings so **it** cannot fly, but **its** wings help **it** to swim very fast.

See **personal writing** if you want to know more.

**in** See **confusing words**: in, inn.

# indefinite articles

The words *a* and *an* are called *indefinite articles* because they do not point to particular things.

**A** red car      **An** old house

These phrases could mean *any* red car or *any* old house.

**The** old house burned down.

The word *the* points to a particular old house. *The* is called the *definite article*.

If you want to know more, see **a, an** and **a, the**.

# indirect speech

Indirect speech is when a writer reports what someone has said but does not write the words that were actually said. Indirect speech is also called *reported speech.*

Anna said that **she will meet us at the movies**. In this sentence we know the meaning of what Anna said but not the words Anna actually said.

Anna said, "**I will meet you at the movies**." In this sentence we know the words that Anna actually said. This is called *direct speech*.

To find out more, see dialogue, direct speech, speech and quotation marks (" ").

# infinitive

An infinitive is a verb that does not have a subject. So it does not act as the whole verb in a sentence. It is used alongside another verb.

They began **to eat** the pizza. In this example, *to eat* is an infinitive verb. The main verb in this sentence is *began*. The subject of *began* is *they*. The verb *to eat* does not have a subject.

The word *to* usually comes before an infinitive.
*to go, to run, to speak, to help, to write*

My dog likes **to go** for a walk. My mother stopped **to help** at an accident.

# informal writing

Informal writing is the way you use words when you want to sound relaxed or casual. You usually use informal writing when you know the reader very well and you do not need to worry about being correct or proper.

For examples of formal and informal writing, see formal/informal writing.

# information text

Information text, also called *nonfiction,* is writing that gives a reader information on a topic.

There are many kinds of information texts. The different kinds are called *text types*.

To find out about different kinds of information texts, see text types.

# initials

Initials are the first letters of people's names. You can see initials used in the telephone directory. A person's family name is listed first, often followed by the initials of the person's other names.

> Smith **A A**
> Smith **A B**
> Smith **B D**

Initials are also used in addresses on letters.

> Mr **A A** Smith
> 10 Spring Street
> SPRINGVALE WA 0555

**inn** See **confusing words**: in, inn.

**instruction text** See procedural text.

# interjections

Interjections are words or short phrases that express greetings or strong feelings. They are a kind of exclamation, so they are sometimes followed by an exclamation mark.

Here are some common interjections:

> Ah! Bad luck! Er, Gee! Hello! Hey! Hi! Hmm! Oh, no! OK, Ouch! Wow! Yuk!

Interjections are very useful when you are writing dialogue.

> "**Oh, no!**" screamed Jill.
> "**Hey!** What's the problem?" asked Tom.

**invitations** See letter writing.

125

# irregular verbs

Irregular verbs are verbs that do not have the ending *-ed* for their past tense. Here are some examples:

*do / did / done, go / went / gone, see / saw / seen*

To find a long list of irregular verbs, see **verbs**: irregular verbs.

**-ise, -ize** For the spelling of words like *realise/ realize*, see spelling.

**it's** See **confusing words**: it's, its and contractions.

**its** See **confusing words**: it's, its.

# jargon

Jargon is language used by experts who know a special subject. Teachers, lawyers, carpenters, doctors each have words and phrases they use that most people who do not do those jobs do not understand.

If a doctor is speaking or writing to other doctors, then jargon is useful. The words are a short way of saying exactly what is meant, and the audience understands.

Here is an example of how a computer expert might speak.

> The *Junior Writers Guide* was written in **SGML** to allow **pdf output** of the data as print, digital **stand-alone cross-platform** software or online media.

The words *SGML*, *pdf*, *output*, *stand-alone* and *cross-platform* make more sense to people who understand computers. The sentence doesn't make much sense to 'non-computer' people.

It is not a good idea to use jargon with people who do *not* understand the words you use. It can make them think you are trying to be smarter than they are.

Jargon helps you say what you mean more easily with people who *do* understand the words you use.

# journal

A *journal* is writing that is a record of events. Travellers and scientists sometimes write journals so they can remember what they did and when they did it.

A journal often has an introduction that tells you what the journal is about. It then has notes called *entries*. These entries are written at different times. With each entry, the writer usually records the date or time.

---

**Plant Journal**

I found some seeds in a packet. There was no label on the packet. I wondered what the seeds would grow into.

**Day 1**
I planted several seeds in my garden and watered them. I will water them every day.

**Day 7**
I found a shoot coming through the soil. I watered the ground again.

**Day 8**
I found five more shoots coming up. The first shoot now has two small leaves.

---

**Notes on style:**

• Most of the verbs in journal entries are in the past tense (*found*, *planted*, *watered*) because the writer is recording what has already happened.
• The writer uses the pronoun *I* because a journal is personal writing.
• The entries are in chronological order (in order of time).
• The entries are usually short notes.

A journal is different from a diary. A journal is usually meant to be read by others, but a diary is usually very private and is meant only for the writer.

To find out more, see **chronological order**, **diary** and **personal writing**.

# journalism

Journalism is the types of writing used in newspapers and magazines. The writers are called *journalists*.

Journalists write in different styles for different sections of a newspaper or magazine. Here are some of the types of writing you can find in a newspaper.

### Latest news (recount of daily events)

Journalists write about things that have happened around the world that day. This writing is a kind of recount text. It gives facts about one event.

Journalists write stories and then give them to the editors. When the editors put the newspaper together, they must fit news stories with advertisements. They cannot trim the advertisements, so they trim the news.

Journalists write the most important details first. Each part of the story is in one sentence. Often a paragraph is only one sentence long. So, if the editor needs to trim the story, the last paragraph is cut first. This means the most important information is still there.

The first paragraph tells the reader the main details. It is called the *lead* or the *banner text*. The journalist tells the reader:

- **Who** the story is about
- **Where** and **when** it happened
- **What** happened
- **How** and **why** it happened

Even if the editor cuts out all except the first paragraph, you will still know the main facts about the news event.

Here is an example of a short news story showing where an editor might trim parts from the end. Notice how the journalist and the editors get your attention with the *headline* and tell you the main facts in the *lead*.

**CHILDREN SPELLBOUND AT SCHOOL**

The grade five children at Seaside School set a new record in a spelling competition this week when they won an international 'spelling bee' on the Internet.

✂.......................................................................

Over three thousand schools from ten different countries around the world entered the competition.

✂.......................................................................

The children spelled 349 words correctly in the international spelling test to become the winners.

✂.......................................................................

Their teacher, Ms Evaliniana Hatzistananasiadopolous, said, "My class became keen on spelling when they learned to spell my name."

✂.......................................................................

The prize for winning the competition was a set of dictionaries.

For more about this style of writing, see recount.

**Feature article (report)**

A feature article is an information report. It gives more information than a news story. The journalist might report on events that happened over a long time.

A feature article might include:
• information about the history of a topic
• an interview with an expert on the topic
• a chart or diagram that explains the topic
• quotations from experts

The main parts of a feature article are:
• **headline** to announce the report
• **introduction** or **lead** to describe the topic
• **middle** to give the main details on the topic
• **ending** to summarise the information

For more about this text type, see report.

(Turn the page for more about journalism. →)

a
b
c
d
e
f
g
h
i
j
k
l
m
n
o
p
q
r
s
t
u
v
w
x
y
z

### Editorial (argument and opinion by the editor)

There is a section of a newspaper where the editor gives an opinion on news topics. The *editorial* might give some facts, but its purpose is to give readers an opinion about the topic.

The main parts of an editorial are:
- **introduction** to say what the topic is
- **opinion** to say what the editor thinks about the topic
- **information** as evidence for the opinion
- **ending** to summarise the opinion or point of view

To find out more about this text type, see argument.

### Letters (views and arguments from readers)

Readers of newspapers often write letters to the editor giving their opinions on a topic. The editor puts some of these in a special section. For an example of a letter to the editor, see argument.

### Advertisements (persuasive argument)

Newspapers earn money by selling advertisements. People advertise in newspapers because they want to persuade readers to buy something or do something.

To find out how to write like this, see advertisement.

**key** See **confusing words**: key, quay.

**knew** See **confusing words**: knew, new.

**knight** See **confusing words**: knight, night and WORD HISTORIES: knight.

**knit** See **confusing words**: knit, nit.

**knot** See **confusing words**: knot, not.

**laid** See **confusing words**: laid, lay, lie.

**lay** See **confusing words**: laid, lay, lie.

**learn** See **confusing words**: learn, teach.

# legend

A *legend* is a story handed down from the past about the adventures of heroes. The story could be true or invented.

Some famous legendary characters and stories from around the world are:

Robin Hood (England)
William Tell (Europe)
Johnny Appleseed (USA)
The Man from Snowy River (Australia)

The heroes in legends are normal but brave people. They do not have magical powers.

To find out about a different type of hero tale, see myth.

Some legends explain why natural things happen, for example, *Why the Moon Changes Shape*. See folktale.

**lend** See **confusing words**: borrow, lend, loan.

**less** See **confusing words**: fewer, less.

# letter writing

Letter writing is also called *correspondence.* It is the way people communicate most in writing. Most correspondence is by letter, greeting card, fax or email.

The style of writing in a letter depends on:
• Why you are writing
• Whom you are writing to
• How well you know the person you are writing to

A letter normally has these parts:
• **Address** of the writer and the **date** it is written
• A **greeting** (*Hi..., Dear...*)
• The **body** of the letter that is the message
• A **closing** (*Love, Best wishes, Yours faithfully*)
• A **signature** (the writer's name)

### Addressing an envelope

Letters are sorted by machines in the post office. This is how you should address an envelope so sorting machines can read it.

```
Sender:
J Brown
25 Coral St
BRIGHTON SA 0555


            Miss M Heron
            390 Sandy Rd
            MT PLEASANT WA 0666
```

### Notes on style:
• Write your own address in the top-left corner or on the back of the envelope.
• Do not use punctuation (full stops, commas).
• Keep the lines and the left-hand column straight.
• Use capital letters in the bottom line.
• Use a dark-coloured pen.
• Do not underline anything.

## Personal letters

Personal letters are to friends and family. You would normally use informal language in a personal letter because you can relax and be more casual with people you feel close to. Even so, there is a way that all letters are normally set out.

> J Brown
> 25 Coral St
> BRIGHTON SA 0555
>
> 16 Sep 2006
>
> Hi Maria
>
> Last night was a drama. I was nearly run over on the road! I was walking across to the deli when a car came speeding around the bend in the road near my house.
>
> I couldn't see the car, and the driver couldn't see me until the last minute. Luckily I stepped back in time and the driver swerved and missed me.
>
> That part of the road has always been a problem. I think I'll write to the council and see if I can get some safety signs put there.
>
> What's happening in your life? I hope you're not having dramas like me!
> Lots of love
> Jimmy xxxooo
> PS I've started taking guitar lessons. Wow!

### Notes on style:
- The writer's address is at the top. It can be on the left- or right-hand side of the page.
- The greeting (*Hi*) is informal.
- The contractions (*couldn't, I'll, you're*) are informal.
- The closing (*Lots of love*) and nickname (*Jimmy*) are informal.
- Symbols for kisses and hugs (*xxxooo*) are informal.
- The use of an interjection (*Wow!*) in the PS is informal.

(Turn the page for more about letter writing. →)

a b c d e f g h i j k l m n o p q r s t u v w x y z

**a
b
c
d
e
f
g
h
i
j
k
l
m
n
o
p
q
r
s
t
u
v
w
x
y
z**

## Business letters

Business letters are to people that you usually do not know as well as friends and family. You would normally use formal language because you want your letter to be taken seriously.

---

J Brown
25 Coral St
BRIGHTON SA 0555

16 Sep 2006

Ms Carol Gates,
Brighton Town Hall

**Subject: Dangerous bend in Coral Street**
Dear Ms Gates,

I wish to bring to your notice a bend in Coral Street that is a danger to pedestrians.

Last night, I was nearly hit by a motorist as I tried to cross the road near my house. I had been careful to look both ways before crossing, but the bend in the road and some bushes on the roadside make it impossible to see cars until they are upon you.

We have many children crossing at this danger spot to go to school. Before someone is killed, I suggest that the Brighton Council place pedestrian warning signs to drivers at the bend.

I hope something can be done about this soon.

Yours truly,
James Brown

---

### Notes on style:
- Sender's address and date is in the top-right corner.
- Receiver's address is on the left margin.
- The subject of the letter is shown in a heading.
- The greeting (*Dear...*,), signature (*Yours truly*) and name (*James Brown*) are formal.
- The writer begins with the problem and then suggests how the problem should be solved.

## Invitations

An invitation is a short letter inviting someone to do something. Invitations are short — they give information about **who**, **what**, **where**, **when** and **why**.

---

### PARTY!

To: **Sam Lukovic**

It's **Rebecca Lang's** birthday party and you are invited!

When? *1 pm-4 pm on Saturday, 7 July*

Where? *15 Oak Street, Hilton*

RSVP by *1 July*

*Rebecca Lang*

*15 Oak St, Hilton WA 0666*

---

### Notes on style:
- The invitation says what the event is about.
- The invitation says where and when the event is.
- The personal name of the guest is used.
- The time, date and place of the event are given.
- Information for a reply (*RSVP*) is given at the end.

### RSVP

An RSVP is a reply to an invitation. An informal RSVP might be made by telephone, email or fax with a simple 'Yes' or 'Sorry, I can't make it' written on the invitation. A formal RSVP would be a short letter. It is impolite to not send an RSVP to an invitation.

To find out where the letters RSVP came from, see WORD HISTORIES: RSVP.

**liar** See **confusing words**: liar, lyre.

**lie** See **confusing words**: laid, lay, lie.

a
b
c
d
e
f
g
h
i
j
k
l
m
n
o
p
q
r
s
t
u
v
w
x
y
z

# limerick

A limerick is a special type of funny poem.

To find out how to write a limerick, see humour.

# lists

A list is a way of writing several ideas so they are easy to read. A list might be things you need to remember to buy at a shop. It can also be ideas about a topic.

Here is an example of a list.

> For this art project you will need:
> - a sheet of white art paper
> - a small paintbrush
> - a set of watercolour paints and some water
> - a small white plastic tray for mixing colours

**Notes on style:**

- A list begins with a heading or opening phrase that tells what the list is about.
- An opening phrase ends with a colon (:).
- The list items can be words, phrases or sentences.
- The list items often begin with pointers such as hyphens, bullet points or numbers.
- Some people begin each item with a capital letter.

**Bullet point lists**

> Wetlands are important because:
> - They are breeding places for fish and other animals,
> - They are feeding grounds for many birds, and
> - They clean the water before it reaches the sea.

**Numbered lists**

If list items need to be read in a special order, then it is a good idea to number each item. Here is an example.

> **Instructions for making this model plane**
> 1. Unclip all the plastic parts.
> 2. Glue part A to part B to make the body.
> 3. Glue parts C and D together and parts E and F together to make the main wings and tail section.
> 4. Glue the tail section and wings to the body.

# literature

Literature is writing that becomes part of a people's culture. It includes narratives and nonfiction.

Literature can be poetry, novels, plays, traditional tales, picture books, reference books or history books.

When a book is published, a copy is sent to the national library where it is kept as part of the literature collection and culture of the country. State libraries also keep a collection of everything published in that region.

For more information, see traditional literature.

**loan** See **confusing words**: borrow, lend, loan and loan, lone.

**lone** See **confusing words**: loan, lone.

**loose** See **confusing words**: loose, lose.

**lose** See **confusing words**: loose, lose.

# lower case

Lower case is the name for the small form of letters in the alphabet. The larger form of letters is called *upper case* or *capital letters*.

**Lower-case letters**

a b c d e f g h i j k l m n o p q r s t u v w x y z

**Upper-case letters**

A B C D E F G H I J K L M N O Q R S T U V W X Y Z

**lyre** See **confusing words**: liar, lyre.

# lyric

A lyric is the words to a song. A lyrical poem sounds like a song when you say it. It can often be set to music. Sometimes a songwriter will change the poem slightly so it makes a better song.

Here is a verse from a traditional counting poem.
Said the first little chick with a quick little squirm,
"I wish I could find a fat little worm."

Here is the same verse rewritten as a lyric for a song.
Said the first little chick with a quick little squirm,
I wish I could find a fat little worm, a fat little worm,
I wish I could find a fat little worm.

In the lyric to the song, some words in the poem were repeated so it would work better to music.

**mail** See **confusing words**: mail, male.

**main** See **confusing words**: main, mane.

**male** See **confusing words**: mail, male.

**mane** See **confusing words**: main, mane.

**many** See **confusing words**: many, much.

**mare** See **confusing words**: mare, mayor.

**may** See **confusing words**: can, may.

**mayor** See **confusing words**: mare, mayor.

## measures

Measures are the way we say how hot or cold, long or short, heavy or light something is. A measure has a name (*metre*, *inch*, *kilogram*, *degree Celsius*, *degree Fahrenheit*, *pound*) to say what kind of measure it is. It has a number to say how much or how many it is.

5 metres          80 kilograms

**Abbreviations**

The names used for measures can be abbreviated. You use these abbreviations only when you write them with numerals. You might do this often in nonfiction writing.

The temperature today reached **24°C**.
The wind speed reached **75 km/h** in the storm.
The mountain is over **7,000 m** high.

For a list of abbreviations for measures, see **abbreviations**: Abbreviations in measures and numbers.

**meat** See **confusing words**: meat, meet.

**medal** See **confusing words**: medal, meddle.

**meddle** See **confusing words**: medal, meddle.

**meet** See **confusing words**: meat, meet.

# metaphor

A metaphor is a way writers build a word picture by making you think of something as if it is something else.

At sunset the clouds **became a giant fire**.
In this sentence, the words *became a giant fire* are a metaphor. The clouds are not really a fire, but the metaphor makes you compare them to a fire.

Metaphors are useful in fiction, poetry and nonfiction writing. Here are some more examples of metaphors:

In the morning, birds are **nature's alarm clock**.
The camel is **the ship of the desert**.
The wheat farmer grows **fields of gold**.

See simile to find another way to build word pictures.

**meter** See **confusing words**: meter, metre.

**metre** See **confusing words**: meter, metre.

**much** See **confusing words**: many, much.

# myth

Myths are stories that have superhuman characters, such as gods and heroes. Myths are often ancient tales that were told to explain natural things. All cultures had tales like this. Here are some examples:

Australian Aboriginal Dreamtime tales (explain many things about animals, people and the world)
Why there are scratches on the Devil's Tower (Native American tale)
*The Sun Chariot* (This Greek tale tells why there are so many deserts in North Africa)

Many modern superhero tales are based on the same pattern as the ancient hero tales. The hero begins life as an orphan, floats across water or space, is adopted and raised by someone and then grows into a powerful, magical, brave fighter of evil.

To find out more about ancient tales, see **folktale** and **legend**.

# names

Careful writers make sure that they spell the name of a person, a place or a business correctly. People usually have strong feelings about their names.

Most people have a *family name* and one or more *given names*. In places like Europe, America, Australia, New Zealand and South Africa, most people write their given names first and their family name last.

**James Adam** (given names) **King** (family name)

In many Asian cultures, people write their family name first and then their given names.

**Lim** (family name) **Su Ling** (given names)

(Turn the page for more about names. →)

140

### Capital letters

The names of particular people, places and organisations begin with a capital letter.

**E**lizabeth **M**ary **F**oster
**B**remerton
**S**mith's **S**upermarket

For more information about capitals and names, see **nouns**: Proper nouns (Special names of things).

### Initials

A person's given names are sometimes abbreviated to the first letter of each name. This is called an *initial*.

Elizabeth **M** Foster    **T J** Smith

Initials are often used on envelopes and in lists such as a telephone directory.

### Nicknames

Nicknames are special names or shortened names given to a person by family or friends.

**Fred** or **Freddy** (short for *Frederick*)
**Sam** (short for *Samantha* and *Samuel*)
**Beaver** (for someone who works hard)

Use nicknames mainly in informal writing to people you know.

### Titles

Titles are words that tell you whether a person is a boy, girl, man, woman or a person with a special position. Here are some titles we use with people's names:
- **Captain** abbreviated to **Capt** (for the captain of a ship)
- **Doctor** abbreviated to **Dr** (for a person who is a doctor or has a university degree called a *doctorate*)
- **Master** (for a boy)
- **Miss** (for a girl)
- **Mister** abbreviated to **Mr** (for a man)
- **Mistress** pronounced /missus/ abbreviated to **Mrs** (for a married woman)
- **Ms** pronounced /muhz/ (for a woman)

Titles always begin with a capital letter when used with a person's name.

a b c d e f g h i j k l m n o p q r s t u v w x y z

# narrative

Narrative is writing that tells a story in fiction, nonfiction or poetry.

A narrative has a beginning, a middle and an end.
• The beginning tells **who** or **what** the story is about and **where** and **when** it happened.
• The middle tells **what** happened to the characters.
• The end summarises what happened and **why**.

When you plan to write a narrative, there are five main things you might think about.

1. **Characters**
Characters are the people, animals or things that the story is about. In a good narrative, the reader feels that the characters are believable. For ideas on characters for your narrative writing, see character.

2. **Setting**
The setting is the place and time that the story happens. In a good narrative, readers get a clear picture of where the story is happening. For ideas of how to create settings, see setting.

3. **Plot**
The plot tells the reader all the things that happen to the characters and the order in which they happen. In a good narrative, the plot must make sense. It would not make sense, for example, if the writer tells you the answer to a mystery but forgets to tell you the clues.

4. **Style**
Style is the way you use language to tell the story. You might write a poem, a play or a biography.

5. **Theme**
The theme is the idea that the narrative is all about. For example, in a fable, the moral of the story is the theme.

Here are some different ways you can write a narrative. For fiction, see anecdote, fable, fairytale, fantasy, folktale, parable and play script.

For nonfiction, see biography and journalism.

For poetry, see ballad, lyric and narrative poem.

# narrative poem

A narrative poem is any poem that tells a story. It does not matter whether the poem is long or short.

Some famous narrative poems are:

*The Pied Piper of Hamelin* by Robert Browning
*The Tale of Custard the Dragon* by Ogden Nash
*Mr Froggie Went A-Courtin'* Anonymous
*A Snake Yarn* by W T Goodge

For two examples of narrative poems, see ballad and cautionary tale.

**naval** See **confusing words**: naval, navel.

**navel** See **confusing words**: naval, navel.

# negatives

Negatives are words that mean 'no'. These words are used to make negative sentences. Some examples are:

*never*, *no*, *nobody*, *none*, *nothing*, *not*

**Never** ride a bicycle unless you wear a helmet.
There was **nothing** inside the box.

For more information about negatives, see double negative. Also, look up contractions for words ending with *n't*.

**neither** See **confusing words**: either, neither.

**new** See **confusing words**: knew, new.

a
b
c
d
e
f
g
h
i
j
k
l
m
n
o
p
q
r
s
t
u
v
w
x
y
z

# newspapers

Newspapers publish the daily news and other information that people find useful each day. The style of writing in a newspaper changes depending on the section it is in.

Here are some of the sections and kinds of writing that might be in a newspaper.

**Nonfiction** (daily events, feature articles, sports reports, weather reports)

**Opinions** (editorials, reviews of books, movies and plays, letters to the editor)

**Fiction** (entertaining cartoons, comic strips)

**Persuasion** (advertisements)

People who write for newspapers are called *journalists*.

To find out how journalists write, see journalism.

**nicknames** See names.

**night** See **confusing words**: knight, night.

**nit** See **confusing words**: knit, nit.

# nonfiction

Nonfiction is writing that gives information or points of view. An author usually must do research, take notes and check that information is correct. The information is then organised to suit the way the reader will use it.

Nonfiction often has graphs, charts, diagrams, maps and photographs to help the reader understand the information or to read it in another way.

Nonfiction writers choose a type of writing to suit their audience and reason for writing. Here are some nonfiction text types and why you might use them.

### Argument

In an argument text, the writer gives an opinion about a topic with information or evidence to support the opinion. Advertisements, reviews and letters to the editor are all arguments. For more, see argument.

### Explanation

An explanation describes how something happens. How a baker makes bread and how bees make honey are explanation topics. For details, see explanation.

### Procedural text

In a procedural text, the writer tells the reader how to make or do something. Recipes, computer manuals and instructions to games are procedural texts. To find out how to write like this, see procedural text.

### Recount

A recount text tells the reader about events that have happened in the past. Autobiographies, biographies, diaries, journals and news stories are all recounts. To find out how to write like this, see recount.

### Report

A report gives facts on a topic and organises the facts so they make sense and are easy to find. To find out about different ways this is done, see report.

# nonsense

Nonsense poems and stories are funny simply because they make no sense: they are ridiculous. This poem is nonsense because the ideas in each line cannot be true: one part undoes the other.

> I went to the movies tomorrow,
> And took a front seat at the back.
> I fell from the floor to the ceiling,
> And broke a front bone in my back.
>
> *Anon.*

In the next example, the conversation is silly because the characters say nothing that makes sense.

### What's for Breakfast?

"What can we eat for breakfast?" asked Sara.

"Well, if we had some ham, we could have ham and eggs, if we had some eggs," said Sam.

"What can we cook it in?" asked Sara.

"We could use the frying pan that I gave away."

"And when will it be ready to eat?" asked Sara.

"Yesterday morning," said Sam.

Sara walked out the locked door.

"Where are you going?" asked Sam.

"For a walk. I'm so full I couldn't eat another thing."

To find out more about funny texts, see humour.

**not** See **confusing words**: knot, not and negatives.

# note-taking

Note-taking means writing short notes on information and ideas you might find useful later. It is an important part of doing research for writing.

Here are some hints about note-taking.

### Skimming

Skim read a paragraph of information and jot down the key words. These key words remind you of the main idea. Add some other words that remind you of details about that idea. Later, rewrite these words into your own sentences. This is a way of making sure you write these ideas in your own words.

### Quoting

Sometimes you want to remember a whole phrase or sentence. If you copy it from a book, then put quotation marks at the beginning and end of the words you have copied. In brackets, write the name of the writer whose words you have copied. This is a way of reminding yourself that these words belong to another writer. It is wrong to use another writer's words without saying where they came from. For details about this, see plagiarism and quotation marks (" ").

### Underlining

If you have a copy of text that you can mark up, it can be a good idea to underline key words and ideas.

### Organising

Sort the ideas and key words you gather under headings about your topic. This helps you to see which ideas belong together in a paragraph or chapter in your writing. It makes it easier to write your first draft.

To find out how note-taking fits into a writing project, see writing process.

# nouns

Nouns are words used to name people, places, things and ideas. There are different types of nouns.

### Abstract nouns (Ideas, feelings and thoughts)

Abstract nouns are the names of ideas, feelings and thoughts — things we can think about or imagine but cannot touch. They are also called *common nouns*.

He had a terrible **fear** of spiders, but with **bravery** and **cleverness** he made it through the tunnel. The **mystery** was solved and **peace** came to the village.

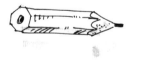

### Collective nouns (Names of groups)

Collective nouns are the names of groups of animals, people or things.

*Animals*: flock (of sheep, birds), herd (of cattle), pride (of lions), school (of fish)
*People*: class, choir, committee, crowd, family, team
*Things*: bunch (of grapes), fleet (of ships)

To find out how to use collective nouns in a sentence, see agreement and collective nouns.

### Common nouns (General names of things)

Common nouns are the general names of people, places, things, feelings and ideas. They do not have a capital letter unless they begin a sentence.

*People*: boy, child, girl, man, woman
*Places*: city, river, galaxy, town, mountain
*Things*: building, computer, dog, pencil
*Feelings and ideas*: dream, happiness, hunger

### Proper nouns (Special names of things)

Proper nouns are the names of particular things. They begin with a capital letter.

*Animals*: Fido the dog, Fluffy the cat
*People*: Dr Clark, Gurmit Singh, Peter
*Places*: Adelaide, South America, Mars, Mount Etna
*Things*: Eiffel Tower, Qantas, London Bridge

# novel

A novel is a long story that comes from the writer's imagination; it is fiction. Novels are written to entertain readers. They are a kind of narrative.

Although novels are fiction, writers often get ideas for a novel from true events. A very old novel is *Robinson Crusoe* by Daniel Defoe, published in 1719. It is the story of a sailor who is shipwrecked and alone on an island for many years. Daniel Defoe got the idea for this story from a report of a man named Alexander Selkirk, who was left alone on a small island for over four years.

A novel is usually about characters who meet a problem. The story tells of events that show how they deal with the problem. Usually the characters learn things and change because of their experience.

To make a novel interesting, the writer must invent interesting characters and settings. The events or the plot of the story need to make the reader want to read more and find out what happens. The writer can choose from different styles of writing to tell the story. You can find out more about this if you look up character, setting, plot and style.

Here are some different kinds of novels.

• **Fantasy**: There is an imaginary world (once upon a time) and characters with magical powers. The good characters face evil characters. Can they use their powers and cleverness to make good win over evil?

• **Historical fiction**: You are taken back into the past. The characters face a problem, which they have to solve without the modern inventions we have today.

• **Mystery**: There is a crime, suspects, clues, the scene of the crime and a detective. Who did it? A story like this is often called a 'whodunit'.

• **Romance**: People meet and fall in love, but then have some problems. Will it be a happy ending?

• **Science fiction**: A strange world of technology is created. The characters face a problem. Can they use science to find a way to survive?

a
b
c
d
e
f
g
h
i
j
k
l
m
**n**
o
p
q
r
s
t
u
v
w
x
y
z

# numbers

Numbers can be written as numerals (figures) or words.

(numerals) 59, 123
(words) fifty-nine, one hundred and twenty-three

### Numerals (figures)

Numerals are used more often in nonfiction writing, especially for letter writing, dates, time, large numbers, money and measures.

Usually you do not begin a sentence with a numeral.

### Words

Two-word numbers between twenty-one and ninety-nine are always joined by a hyphen.

For more information about numbers, see addresses on letters, dates, measures and time.

# numerical order

Numerical order means 'in order of numbers'. This is a way of organising information in your writing. It is mainly used in nonfiction. For example, the rules for playing a game are often written in numerical order.

For more ideas on how to organise information, see order.

**oar** See **confusing words**: oar, or, ore.

**-oes, -os** To find out whether to add *-es* or *-s* to words ending with the letter *o*, see plural.

**of** See **confusing words**: of, off.

**off** See **confusing words**: of, off.

# OK, okay

Both of these spellings are correct.

**one** See **confusing words**: one, won.

# only

Write the word *only* as near as possible to the word or phrase you want it to describe.

See how the meaning changes as the word *only* moves in this sentence.

**Only** I talked with my friend for an hour.
I **only** talked with my friend for an hour.
I talked with **only** my friend for an hour.
I talked with my **only** friend for an hour.
I talked with my friend for **only** an hour.

# onomatopoeia

Onomatopoeia (pronounced *on-uh-mat-uh-**pee**-yuh*) means 'words that mean what they sound like'. Writers use onomatopoeia to make their writing sound interesting. Here are some onomatopoeic words:

*bang, boom, buzz, crash, hiss, miaow, moo, quack, roar, snap, snarl, snore, splash, whoosh*

Onomatopoeia is used a lot in the song *Old MacDonald Had a Farm*.

a
b
c
d
e
f
g
h
i
j
k
l
m
n
o
p
q
r
s
t
u
v
w
x
y
z

**or** See **confusing words**: oar, or, ore.

# order

Writers need to organise information in their writing into an order that makes sense to the reader. They think about this at the planning stage of their writing.

Here are some of the ways you can organise your nonfiction writing.

### Alphabetical order

Alphabetical order means 'in the order of the alphabet'. Writers use alphabetical order when they have lots of headings and they want the reader to be able to find the headings easily. A dictionary and an encyclopedia list headings in alphabetical order. Words or headings are listed by their first letter, then the second letter and so on. For example:

**aa**rdvark
**an**t
**b**eetle
**c**aterpillar

The red headwords in this *Junior Writers Guide* are in alphabetical order.

### Chronological order

Chronological order means 'in order of time'. Writers use chronological order in a diary or journal. The headings are in order of dates when things happen.

The events in a story are usually in chronological order from the beginning to the ending.

### Numerical order

Numerical order means 'in order of the numbers'. Writers use numerical order when they want the reader to do something in correct stages. The instructions in a recipe or an art or craft activity are often numbered. This shows which instruction is done first, second and so on.

**ore** See **confusing words**: oar, or, ore.

**our** See **confusing words**: hour, our.

**pail** See **confusing words**: pail, pale.

**pain** See **confusing words**: pain, pane.

**pair** See **confusing words**: pair, pear.

**pale** See **confusing words**: pail, pale.

**pane** See **confusing words**: pain, pane.

# parable

A parable is a short story that teaches a lesson about the right way to live or behave. The characters in parables are usually ordinary people. This makes readers think that the story could be about them.

---

### The Bully at the Fountain

One hot day, a bully pushed a smaller child out of his way to be the first to drink at the water fountain.

Some water had spilled onto the ground. The bully slipped on the water, fell and hurt himself. The smaller child helped the bully to get up from the ground.

"Why are you helping me?" asked the bully.

"It is better that I treat people well," said the child. "I will never make friends if I treat people badly."

---

To find out about other stories that teach a lesson, see allegory, cautionary tale and fable.

# paragraphs

A paragraph is a section of writing that is about one particular idea in that writing. Writers use paragraphs to organise ideas in writing. This makes a text easier for readers to understand.

A paragraph can have just one sentence. In a newspaper, many paragraphs are only one sentence. For more about newspaper writing see journalism.

A paragraph can have several sentences. It usually has three main parts:

- **A topic sentence**: This tells the reader what the paragraph is about. It also helps the writer to stick to that topic in the rest of the paragraph.
- **Details**: This can be a few sentences that give information about the topic of the paragraph.
- **A summary sentence**: This sentence reminds the reader of the main points made about the topic.

Here is an example.

> The zebra is a wild horse. Unlike other horses, it has black and white stripes all over its body. On each zebra, these markings are unique; they are different from every other zebra. Also, unlike domestic horses, the hair on a zebra's mane sticks straight up from its neck. There are only two types of wild horse left in the world, so the zebra is very special.

**Notes on style:**
- The **topic** of this paragraph is *the zebra is a wild horse*.
- The **detail** sentences compare the zebra to other horses in colour, markings and mane.
- The last sentence gives a **summary** of the topic by saying how special the zebra is as a wild horse.

Other points to remember:
- You can indent paragraphs (begin the first word in a little from the margin) or leave a space between them.
- A paragraph should not be too long. Most paragraphs have about two to ten sentences.

**parentheses** See brackets ( ).

# parody

*Parody* is writing that makes fun of a well-known story, poem or song. Writers often use characters and familiar words from the old story. Here is an example.

---

### LITTLE RED RIDING HOODLUM

Once upon a time, Mr Wolf was strolling through the forest, minding his own business, when he met a little girl wearing a red riding jacket with a red hood.

"Oh, Mr Wolf," she cried sweetly. "I need to get this basket of goodies to my poor grandma at the end of the forest. Would you rush it to her, please? I'll give you six juicy chickens for your dinner if you do."

"Yes, I'll do that," said Mr Wolf, "but where are my chickens?"

"I'll give them to you when you return," she said.

So Mr Wolf rushed the basket to Grandma's house and then ran back to the forest.

"OK, Grandma has the basket. Where are my chickens?" asked Mr Wolf.

"Oh, Mr Wolf!" said the girl. "What big teeth you have. They scare me so. Can you please close your mouth?" So Mr Wolf closed his mouth.

"Oh, Mr Wolf! What big eyes you have. They scare me so. Can you please close them?" So Mr Wolf closed his eyes.

"Oh, Mr Wolf! What big ears you have. Can you please cover them?" So Mr Wolf placed his paws over his ears. He could not see, hear or speak.

Mr Wolf waited for a long time, but nothing happened. At last, he opened his eyes. The little girl in the red riding jacket and red hood had disappeared.

"I've been hoodwinked!" cried Mr Wolf. "Cheated! Swindled and duped! Just wait until I meet that Little Red Riding Hoodlum again."

---

For another example of parody, see humour.

# participles

Participles are forms of verbs. There are two types.

**Present participles** (verbs that end with *-ing*)
*starting, eating, falling, sleeping, shouting, saying, wanting, having, feeling, thinking, hoping, wishing*

**Past participles** (verbs that usually end with *-ed* or *-t*)
*started, slept, shouted, wanted, felt, hoped, wished*

Some past participles do not end with *-ed* or *-t*.
*eaten, fallen, said, had, thought*

For more examples of past participles that do not end with *-ed* or *-t*, see **verbs**: Irregular verbs.

# parts of speech

To make a sentence we use different types of words. Each type plays a different part in making meaning. These different word types are called 'parts of speech'.

There are nine parts of speech:
- **nouns** (words that name people, places and things — *child, Peter, home, London, dog, planet*)
- **pronouns** (words that can be used in place of nouns — *I, me, we, us, you, he, him, she, her, it, they, them*)
- **adjectives** (words that describe nouns — *red, big, old, good, angry*)
- **articles** (words that point to nouns — *a, an, the*)
- **verbs** (words that are about doing, speaking, thinking, feeling, having and being — *eats, jumped, said, wants, had, were, is*)
- **adverbs** (words that add meaning to verbs by telling how, when or where — *loudly, today, here, there*)
- **conjunctions** and **connectives** (words that connect or join ideas — *and, but, so, because, if, then*)
- **prepositions** (words that show position — *in, out, on*)
- **interjections** (words that express feelings — *ah! ha! hmm! mm! oh! wow! yuk!*)

Find out more by looking these words up in this guide.

**passed** See **confusing words**: passed, past.

**past** See **confusing words**: passed, past.

# past tense

The past tense is any form of a verb we use to express what has already happened. Here are two ways to use the verb *write* in the past tense.

> Yesterday I **wrote** a story.
> I **have written** a story.

To find out more, see tense and verbs.

**paw** See **confusing words**: paw, poor, pore, pour.

**peace** See **confusing words**: peace, piece.

**peal** See **confusing words**: peal, peel.

**pear** See **confusing words**: pair, pear.

**peel** See **confusing words**: peal, peel.

# period

*Period* means 'full stop'. See full stop (.).

**person** See point of view and pronouns.

# personal writing

Personal writing is text written from the writer's point of view. It is usually about personal thoughts, experiences, opinions and beliefs.

Personal letters, journals, diaries, letters to the editor and autobiographies are examples of personal writing.

In personal writing, you often use the pronouns *I*, *me*, *my*, *mine*, *we*, *us*, *our* and *ours*. Here is an example.

> **I** take **my** dog for a walk in the park. He keeps **me** fit because **I** exercise with him every day.

The following example does *not* show you anything personal about the writer. It is *impersonal* writing.

> **People** take **their** dogs for a walk in the park. **It** keeps **them** fit because **they** exercise every day.

For more information, see impersonal writing.

# personification

*Personification* in writing is when writers make animals or things seem human. This can make the reader have feelings for an animal character or an object like a robot.

---

**Rodney Robot**

When Jay had finished fitting all the old computer pieces into his toy robot, he connected the battery and suddenly the robot came to life.

"Now that's better," said the robot. "I've waited weeks for someone to finally discover the real me."

"Who are you?" asked Jay.

"I'm Rodney. Rodney Robot," he replied.

"Wow! I could show you off at school. The other kids will be amazed!" cried Jay.

"Whoa! Not so fast," interrupted Rodney. "I'm not so sure about that. I think I'd feel a bit embarrassed being held up like a toy. I've got feelings, you know."

Rodney Robot sat back in a small chair, crossed his legs and cast his eyes round the room.

"Hmm! Not a bad place you've got here. Bit of a mess, but I can clean that up."

Clean up the room? Jay was beginning to see some advantages to having Rodney around. What else could he do?

"Are you good at mathematics?" Jay asked.

---

**Notes on style:**

Look for these techniques the writer uses to make Rodney Robot seem human.

- **pronouns** (The writer uses the personal pronouns *he*, *him*, *his* for Rodney instead of the pronoun *it*.)
- **name** (The robot has a human name, 'Rodney'.)
- **feelings** (Rodney has feelings like a person.)
- **actions** (Rodney acts like a person. He sits in a chair and folds his legs.)

# persuasive writing

Persuasive writing is any text that tries to get the reader to do, think or believe something. Advertisements and letters trying to sell you something or get you to agree with an opinion are examples of persuasive writing.

For some examples of persuasive writing, see advertisement and argument.

# phrases

A *phrase* is a group of words that has meaning but is not a sentence. Writers use phrases to add meaning to a sentence.

Here are some phrases:
> the toy robot
> in the old box
> a new battery

These phrases do not make a sentence by themselves, but they can be made into a sentence if a verb is added.
> **The toy robot in the old box** needed **a new battery**.

**piece** See **confusing words**: peace, piece.

# plagiarism

*Plagiarism* means copying another writer's work and pretending it is your own. This is regarded as stealing ideas. If you use another writer's words, then you must tell your readers. You do this by using quotation marks to show the words you have copied. You should also say where you copied them from.

For more information, see quotation marks (" ").

**plain** See **confusing words**: plain, plane.

**plane** See **confusing words**: plain, plane.

# planning

Writers usually plan their writing. They do not just sit down and write. The planning process helps writers to organise their ideas before they write a first draft.

For information on ways to plan your writing, see **writing process**: Project planning.

# plays

Plays are narratives that are acted out in front of an audience. They are a form of drama. Actors play the parts of characters in the story. They learn their parts from a play script.

The most common kinds of plays are:

- **comedy** (a funny story that makes the audience laugh)
- **pantomime** (a funny play based on a famous fairytale, usually performed during a holiday season)
- **romance** (a story in which characters fall in love)
- **tragedy** (a story in which characters meet a sad ending because they are greedy or jealous or have some other fault)

Most cultures have traditional stories that fit these types of plays.

160

# play script

A play script is a text written for actors to perform before an audience. The play might be on stage, radio or TV.

In a play script, the actors who play the parts of the characters tell a story by speaking to each other or the audience. This is called *dialogue*. For examples of the different ways writers use speech, see **dialogue**.

Here is an example of a short play script.

---

### The Mystery of the Missing Monkey

**Cast**
Zookeeper, Boy, Girl, Monkey
**Scene**
*A zookeeper is placing food in the monkey habitat at the zoo. A boy and a girl watch.*
**Zookeeper**: *(Chuckling)* He, he! You just watch. Our monkey will love these goodies for lunch.
**Girl**: But where's the monkey?
**Zookeeper**: He always waits in the trees when I bring food.
**Boy**: What do the monkeys eat?
**Zookeeper**: They like fruit and...um...vegetables. They also...
**Boy**: *(Interrupting)* Hey! There's a hole in that fence around the monkey area. It's over by the...
**Zookeeper**: *(Holding his head)* Oh, no! The monkey is missing. He's escaped!
**Girl**: Wow! That's a really big hole. Maybe he was stolen.
*(The zookeeper rushes off stage.)*

---

Look for these things in the play script:

• **Cast** (The characters in the play are listed at the beginning.)

• **Scene** (The scene is the setting of the story.)

• **Character lines** (The lines are the words to be spoken by each character. The character's name is written at the beginning of each line.)

• **Prompts** (Words in brackets give the actors clues for how to act.)

(Turn the page for more about play scripts.→)

**Notes on style:**
It is important to make the characters sound natural when they speak. Here are some points about style in writing a play script.
- **interjections** (*He, he! Oh, no! Wow!*) These words make the speech sound natural.
- **interruptions** (*It's over by the...*) People often interrupt each other when they talk
- **contractions** (*where's, can't, there's, It's, He's, That's*) People shorten phrases and words in their normal speech.
- **pauses** (*They like fruit and...um...*) People often use words like *um* and *er* to pause while they are thinking.

To find out more about interjections, contractions and dialogue, look up these topics in this guide.

# plot

Plot is the part of a narrative that tells you what happens in a story. It is all the events that make up a story.

Thinking of ideas for a plot and making sure that they are in a sensible order is an important part of planning.

The plot of a story has a **beginning**, a **middle** and an **end** or conclusion.
- In the **beginning**, the writer introduces the characters and describes the setting.
- In the **middle**, the writer introduces a problem for the characters and describes events that show how the characters try to solve the problem.
- The events often build in excitement towards a crisis. The reader wonders if the problem will be solved.
- In the **end**, the writer invents a clever or surprise event that shows how the characters solved the problem.

To find out more about plot and other parts of a narrative, see narrative.

# plural

The word *plural* means 'more than one'. The word *singular* means 'just one'. Nouns, pronouns and verbs have plural forms.

**Plural nouns**

We make the plural of most nouns by changing their ending. The most common way is to add *s* or *es*.

*Adding s*
> one pencil — a set of pencil**s**
> one shoe — a pair of shoe**s**
> one cloud — many cloud**s**
> one house — several house**s**

*Adding es*

We add *es* to nouns that end with *ch*, *sh*, *s*, *ss*, *x* or *z*.
> **ch** — branch**es**, lunch**es**, peach**es**, stitch**es**
> **sh** — bush**es**, brush**es**, dish**es**, rash**es**, wish**es**
> **s** — bus**es**, gas**es**, octopus**es**, virus**es**, walrus**es**
> **ss** — address**es**, class**es**, glass**es**, kiss**es**
> **x** — box**es**, fox**es**, prefix**es**, index**es**
> **z** — quizz**es**, waltz**es**

*Nouns ending with o*

We add *s* to most nouns that end with the letter *o* to make the plural. However, there are a few of these words that have *es* added to make them plural.
> **-s** — cuckoo**s**, kangaroo**s**, memo**s**, piano**s**, radio**s**, silo**s**, solo**s**, studio**s**
> **-es** — echo**es**, hero**es**, potato**es**, tomato**es**, tornado**es**

A few words that end with the letter *o* can have either *s* or *es* to make them plural.
> banjo**s** or banjo**es**
> dingo**s** or dingo**es**
> halo**s** or halo**es**
> mosquito**s** or mosquito**es**
> zero**s** or zero**es**

(Turn the page for more about plurals. →)

*Nouns ending with y*

If a noun ends with a consonant and *y*, change the *y* to *i* and add *es* to make the plural.

> baby — bab**ies**
> bully — bull**ies**
> butterfly — butterfl**ies**
> dairy — dair**ies**
> family — famil**ies**
> gully — gull**ies**
> lady — lad**ies**
> sky — sk**ies**

If there is a vowel before the *y* ending, add *s* to make the plural.

> boy — boy**s**       key — key**s**
> guy — guy**s**       tray — tray**s**

*Nouns ending with f, ff or fe*

Just add *s* to most nouns ending with *f, ff* or *fe* to make the plural.

> chief — chief**s**
> cliff — cliff**s**
> roof — roof**s**

With a special group of nouns ending with *f* or *fe* you change the ending to *ves* to make the plural.

> calf — cal**ves**       elf — el**ves**       half — hal**ves**
> knife — kni**ves**       leaf — lea**ves**       life — li**ves**
> loaf — loa**ves**       self — sel**ves**       shelf — shel**ves**
> thief — thie**ves**       wife — wi**ves**       wolf — wol**ves**

With a very small group of nouns ending with *f*, you can spell the plural with *s* or *ves*.

> dwarf**s** or dwar**ves**
> hoof**s** or hoo**ves**
> scarf**s** or scar**ves**
> wharf**s** or whar**ves**

*Nouns ending with ful*

If a noun ends with *ful*, add *s* to make the plural.

> Add two **spoonfuls** of milk to the bowl and then stir.

Other examples are:

> cupful**s**, handful**s**, mouthful**s**

*Exceptions*

A few nouns end with *en* to make the plural.
> child — child**en**
> ox — ox**en**,
> man — m**en**
> woman — wom**en**

A few nouns change their middle to make them plural.
> foot — f**ee**t
> goose — g**ee**se
> tooth — t**ee**th
> louse — l**ice**
> mouse — m**ice**

A few nouns don't change at all to make the plural.
> They caught one **fish** yesterday and two **fish** today.
> He counted one **sheep**, two **sheep** to get to sleep.

Some other examples of nouns that do not normally change to make the plural are:
> deer, dirt, information, shrimp, trout

*Foreign words*

Some English nouns came from foreign languages. You can often tell these words because they end with the letters *is* or *um* or *us* or *a*.

Words ending with *is* often change to *es* for the plural.
> crisis — cris**es**
> oasis — oas**es**

Words ending with *um* often change to *a* for the plural.
> bacterium — bacteri**a**
> maximum — maxim**a**

Words ending with *us* often change to *i* for the plural.
> fungus — fung**i**
> radius — radi**i**

Some words ending with *a* change to *ae* for the plural.
> antenna — antenn**ae**
> larva — larv**ae**

(Turn the page for more about plurals. →)

a
b
c
d
e
f
g
h
i
j
k
l
m
n
o
**p**
q
r
s
t
u
v
w
x
y
z

## Plural pronouns

Most pronouns have plural forms.

| Singular | Plural |
|----------|--------|
| I | we |
| me | us |
| my | our |
| mine | ours |
| he, she, it | they |
| him, her | them |
| his, her, its | their |
| his, hers | theirs |

The pronouns *you*, *your* and *yours* are the same for both singular and plural.

## Plural verbs

Many verbs have singular and plural forms. You need these to match a singular or plural subject in a sentence. Many singular verbs end with *s* and the plural ends without an *s*. Here is an example:

She **swims** in the morning. (singular)
They **swim** in the afternoon. (plural)

Here are some more examples:

She **likes** to swim.    They **like** to swim.
That dog **barks** a lot.    Those dogs **bark** a lot.

Some verbs have different words for singular and plural. Here are two examples:

- The verb *to be*
  I **am**. She **is**. It **was**. (singular)
  We **are**. They **are**. They **were**. (plural)
- The verb *to have*
  He **has**. She **has**. It **has**. (singular)
  They **have**. (plural)

# poetry

Poetry is writing in which the writer or *poet* expresses ideas by carefully choosing words for their sounds, rhythms and meaning. The piece of writing is called a *poem*. Poets use words to create pictures in the mind of the reader. They also choose words carefully to keep their poem short.

### Sounds of words

There are special techniques poets use with the sounds of words. Some of these techniques are:

- **alliteration** (repeating the beginning sound in words — **Tr**ip-**tr**ap-**tr**ip-**tr**ap, **tr**otting on the **tr**ack.)
- **assonance** (repeating a vowel sound within words — The fluttering butterfly was suddenly gone.)
- **consonance** (repeating a consonant sound within words — **P**redators a**pp**eared; the im**p**ala **p**anicked.)
- **rhyme** (repeating the end sounds of words — The moon at **night**, casts a soft **light**.)
- **rhythm** (creating a pattern of strong and weak beats with words — With a **wink** of his **eye** and a **smile** on his **face**, he would **tell** us a **tale** of a **far**away **place**.)

Other techniques with sounds are onomatopoeia and sibilance.

### Pictures with words

Poets use special techniques to create word pictures. To find out about these techniques, see metaphor and simile.

### Forms of poetry

There are many ways to write poetry. Some poems rhyme at the end of lines, some do not. Some poems are short, some are long. Some have regular patterns, some do not. To find out about different forms of poetry, see ballad, cinquain, couplet, free verse, haiku, limerick and quatrain.

167

# point of view

All narrative writing is told through someone's eyes. It might be a storyteller who is not part of the story. It might be the writer or a character in the story. Each gives a different point of view about a story.

A writer can make you understand the point of view by using certain pronouns.
- Writing in the **first person** uses the pronouns *I*, *me*, *my*, *mine*, *we*, *us* and *our*.
- Writing in the **second person** uses the pronouns *you*, *your* and *yours*.
- Writing in the **third person** uses the pronouns *he*, *him*, *his*, *she*, *her*, *hers*, *it*, *its*, *they*, *them*, *their* and *theirs*.

The following examples show what writing sounds like when the point of view changes.

**First person**
> Just as **I** opened the door, all the lights went out. **I** was alone in a strange house as dark as a cave.

In this example, we know that the story is from the point of view of the writer or a character in the story. The author uses *first-person pronouns*.

**Second person**
> Imagine, **you** open the door and all the lights go out. **You** are alone in a strange house as dark as a cave.

In this example, the author places the reader in the story and makes you imagine a situation from your point of view. The author uses *second-person pronouns*.

**Third person**
> Just as Jason opened the door, all the lights went out. **He** was alone in a strange house as dark as a cave.

In this example, the author tells about a character (Jason) in the story. The author uses *third-person pronouns*.

**poor** See **confusing words**: paw, poor, pore, pour.

**pore** See **confusing words**: paw, poor, pore, pour.

# portmanteau words

Portmanteau (/*port*-**man**-*toe*/) words are words formed by blending a part of one word with a part of another. Here are some examples:

aquarium + aerobics = **aquarobics**
breakfast + lunch = **brunch**
motor + hotel = **motel**
parachute + troop = **paratroop**
smoke + fog = **smog**

**pour** See **confusing words**: paw, poor, pore, pour.

**practice** See **confusing words**: practice, practise.

**practise** See **confusing words**: practice, practise.

**praise** See **confusing words**: praise, prays, preys.

**prays** See **confusing words**: praise, prays, preys.

# predicate

The *predicate* is the part of a sentence that tells you what is being said about the subject of the sentence.

The following sentences are all about the same subject, *Jane*. Notice how the predicate can be just one word (the verb) or several words as more information about the subject is added.

Jane **laughed**.
Jane **laughed loudly**.
Jane **laughed loudly at the joke**.

To find out about the other main part of a sentence, see subject.

a
b
c
d
e
f
g
h
i
j
k
l
m
n
o
p
q
r
s
t
u
v
w
x
y
z

# preface

A preface is information written by the author of a book to explain how or why the book was written. The author might also mention people who helped in some way to develop the book. The preface is usually at the beginning of a book.

# prefixes

Prefixes are word parts added to the beginning of a root word. They change the meaning of the word.

Here are some prefixes that mean 'not'. They change the meaning of a word to the opposite.
- **dis**: disagree, disown
- **il**: illegal, illogical
- **im**: impossible, impatient
- **in**: invisible, insoluble
- **ir**: irregular, irresponsible
- **mis**: misbehave, misunderstanding
- **non**: nonsmoking, nonsense
- **un**: unhelpful, uneasy

Here are some examples of other prefixes.

| Prefix | Means | Examples |
|---|---|---|
| al- | every, all | already, altogether, always |
| bi- | two | bicycle, binoculars, biplane |
| by- | beside | bystander, byway |
| co- | with | cooperate, copilot |
| multi- | many | multicoloured, multicultural |
| post- | after | postdated, postscript |
| re- | again | repay, replace, research, revolve |
| sub- | under | subheading, submarine, submerge |

**Did you know?**
The four prefixes used most in English are **un**-, **re**-, **in**- and **dis**-. About two out of every three words with prefixes begin with these letters.

*above*

*behind*  *beside*

*beneath*

# prepositions

Prepositions are words like *to*, *from*, *with*, *for*, *into* and *between*. They link nouns and pronouns to other words in a sentence. They show the position or place of something.

> He borrowed a book **from** <u>me</u>.

In this example, the preposition *from* is placed before the pronoun *me*.

Here are some other examples:

> **Between** <u>you and me</u>, we can do this job.
> We walked **to** <u>school</u>.
> The train went **under** <u>a bridge</u> and **through** <u>a tunnel</u>.

Here are some other prepositions:

> *above, after, among, around, at, before, beneath, behind, beside, by, down, in, into, near, of, off, on, onto, over, up, upon*

**present participle** See participles.

# present tense

The present tense is the way we write verbs to show events or actions happening now or all the time.

> Right now, I **am reading** a book.
> I **read** fiction and nonfiction every day.
> My friend **reads** a lot too.

The verbs *am reading*, *read* and *reads* are in the present tense.

For more about tenses, see **verbs**: Forms of verbs.

**preys** See confusing words: praise, prays, preys.

**principal** See **confusing words**: principal, principle.

**principle** See **confusing words**: principal, principle.

# procedural text

Procedural texts or instructions show readers how to do or make something. Recipes, computer manuals, 'how to make it' activities, sewing and knitting patterns and rules to games are all procedural texts.

Procedural texts usually have three main parts:

1. An **introduction** that names or describes the topic

2. A **list** of things needed to do the activity

3. **Instructions** to tell the reader what to do

### Instructions in a letter

In this email, an editor gives instructions to an author about how to send a manuscript to a publisher.

---

**To**: g.smith@wave.xxx
**Cc**:
**Subject**: How to submit a manuscript

Dear Mr Smith
To submit a manuscript to Easy Publications you need:
- A list of books you have already had published
- Information about your qualifications
The standard procedure we suggest is:
1. Check our website for information on the kinds of books
   we publish.
2. Check that your manuscript fits the style of our books.
3. Type your manuscript in the body of an email.
4. Address the email to editor@easy.xxx.
Yours truly
Ann Penna
Editor's Assistant

---

**Notes on style:**
- The 'Subject' box describes the topic of the letter.
- The lists show what the author needs to send.
- The writer gives numbered instructions on what to do.

**Rules to a game**

---

### "Film Stars"

Test your knowledge of the film stars.

**You will need**:
• 4 to 10 or more players
• Notepaper and a pen for each player

**Rules**

1. Choose a quizmaster.

2. The quizmaster thinks of the name of a film star and gives you one clue.

3. Take it in turns asking the quizmaster, "Does it have the letter...?" The quizmaster can say only *yes* or *no*.

4. Note the letter so you can remember all the letter clues. Try to guess the name from the letter clues.

6. When it is your turn, you can either ask the quizmaster about another letter or you can tell the quizmaster your guess. You cannot do both in the same turn.

7. At any time you can say "Film star!" and try to guess the name. If you are correct, you become the quizmaster. If you are wrong, you are out of the game until the next round.

---

**Notes on style:**
• It is in the **second person**. The writer speaks directly to you with the pronouns *you* and *your*.
• The writer uses **commands** in the rules. Commands begin with action verbs (*choose*, *take*, *note*).

For more information, see **commands**, **point of view** and **pronouns**.

**profit** See **confusing words**: profit, prophet.

a
b
c
d
e
f
g
h
i
j
k
l
m
n
o
p
q
r
s
t
u
v
w
x
y
z

# pronouns

Pronouns are words you can use in place of nouns that have already been mentioned in your writing.

Some pronouns are:

> *I, me, my, mine, you, your, yours, he, him, his, she, her, hers, it, its, we, us, our, ours, they, them, their, theirs, myself, ourselves, who, whose, which, that*

Here are some ways these words are useful in writing.

### Avoiding overuse of a word

Pronouns are useful when you want to avoid using the same noun or noun phrase too often. Here is what writing might be like if we did not have pronouns:

> **Donna** took **Donna's** shoes off, flopped onto **Donna's** bed and fell asleep before **Donna** had dinner.

Here is the same sentence with pronouns to avoid using the word *Donna* too often.

> Donna took **her** shoes off, flopped onto **her** bed and fell asleep before **she** had dinner.

### Point of view

Pronouns make it possible for you to decide who will tell a story you write. Will it be a character in the story or a storyteller talking about characters in the story? This is called *point of view*. Writers use *first-person*, *second-person* or *third-person* pronouns to do this. To find out more about this, see point of view.

You can find out more about pronouns if you go to case and plural.

# proofreading

Proofreading is the last stage of editing before a piece of writing is published. Proofreaders check the text to see if there are errors in spelling, punctuation and capital letters.

For more information, see writing process.

# proper nouns

Proper nouns are the names of particular people, places and things. They begin with a capital letter.

**A**ngela, **N**ew **Y**ork, **S**aturday, **S**eptember, **E**ngland

For more information about proper nouns, see **nouns**.

**prophet**  See **confusing words**: profit, prophet.

# prose

Prose is ordinary writing or speech that does not have a regular rhythm like most poetry. It also does not have a regular rhyming pattern. Prose is used in both fiction and nonfiction writing.

# proverbs

A proverb is a short, wise saying that has been popular for a long time. Some examples are:

*Make hay while the sun shines.*
*Those who live in glass houses should not throw stones.*
*Don't cry over spilled milk.*

Proverbs are often used as the moral of short stories, such as fables.

**Beware!**

If a proverb is used too much in writing, it can become a cliché. To find out why this is not good for your writing, see **cliché**.

# publishing

To publish means 'to make public'. These are a few of the ways you can publish your writing:

- Display it on a wall or noticeboard
- Put a copy of it in the school library
- Place it on a website on the Internet
- Read it to an audience
- Perform it as a play

To find out about all the stages in the writing process leading up to publication, see writing process.

# pun

A pun is a funny play on words that have the same sound but different meanings (homonyms).

> What did the tree do when the crowd cheered?
> It took a **bough**.

In this example, the pun is with the word *bough*. The meaning in the sentence is that a tree would *bow* like an actor on stage when a crowd cheered.

To find a long list of homonyms you could use to write puns, see confusing words.

To find more ideas for using puns to make people laugh, see humour.

# punctuation

Punctuation is the way we use marks in writing to make the meaning clear. It also shows a reader when to pause or give extra stress to words in sentences.

These are the main punctuation marks. Each mark is described under its own heading in this book.

| apostrophe | ' | exclamation mark | ! |
|---|---|---|---|
| brackets | ( ) | full stop | . |
| bullet point | • | hyphen | - |
| colon | : | question mark | ? |
| comma | , | quotation marks | " " |
| dash | — | semicolon | ; |
| ellipsis points | ... | slash mark | / |

## To make meaning clear

These sentences have the same words but different punctuation and meanings.

She reads **sometimes.** After school she watches television. (She doesn't always read.)
She reads. **Sometimes** after school she watches television. (She doesn't always watch television.)

The dog knows **its** home. (The dog owns the home.)
The dog knows **it's** home. (The dog is home.)

The teacher said, **"Matt is in trouble."**
(Matt has a problem.)
**"The teacher,"** said Matt, **"is in trouble."**
(The teacher has a problem.)

## To show expression

Punctuation marks show how to express words. These sentences have the same words, but you would read each sentence with a different expression.

Oh, that's a problem**.**
Oh**!** That's a problem**!**
Oh**?** That's a problem**?**

177

# quatrain

A quatrain is four lines of rhyming verse. It can be a whole poem or just one verse in a longer poem. Its rhyming pattern can be ABAB or AABB or ABCB.

To find out about rhyming patterns, see **rhyme**.

**quay** See **confusing words**: **key, quay**.

# question mark (?)

The question mark (?) is a punctuation mark used to show that a question is being asked. It tells the reader that words should be read or spoken as a question.

"Where are you going**?**"
"Nowhere."
"Nowhere**?**"
"Well, nowhere special. Why do you ask**?**"

The word *nowhere* in this example is used in both a statement and a question. The only way you know how to read each is by looking at the punctuation marks.

When a question is asked in direct speech, the question mark is placed *inside* the quotation marks.
"Where are you going**?**"

# questions

Questions are sentences that ask for information or action. Questions end with a question mark.

Here are some ways you can write questions.

- Begin with one of the *wh* words (*what, when, where, which, who, whose, why*).
    **What** is the time?
    **Why** do you want to know?

- Begin with part of the verbs *to be*, *to be able (can)*, *to have* or *to do*.
    **Am** I allowed to go?
    **Can** we eat the rest of the cake?
    **Have** they packed their things?
    **Do** they like camping?

- Tag a question onto the end of a statement. Notice how the tag questions can have the word *not* (*n't*) in them.
    I am allowed to go, **aren't I**?
    We can eat the rest of the cake, **can't we**?
    They have packed their things, **haven't they**?

- Put a question mark at the end of a statement. The question mark tells the reader to use his or her voice to make the sentence sound as if it is a question.
    I'm allowed to go**?** You're sure of that**?**

To find out about another kind of question, see rhetorical questions.

**quiet** See **confusing words**: quiet, quite.

**quite** See **confusing words**: quiet, quite.

# quotation marks (" ")

Quotation marks (also called *speech marks* or *inverted commas*) enclose words that are spoken or quoted. They are also used to give special attention to words.

### Words that are spoken

When you write words a character or a person actually says, you place quotation marks at the beginning and the end of the words spoken. The quotation marks enclose the speech.

**"Where are you?"** asked Dad.

The words *Where are you?* were spoken. The words *asked Dad* tell you who spoke.

The spoken words can be at the end of a sentence.

Helena replied, **"I'm cleaning my room."**

### Words that are quoted

Sometimes in your writing, you repeat or use words that someone else has spoken or written. This is called a *quotation*. You must always place quotation marks at the beginning and the end of words you have quoted.

The writing on the statue said that it was **"the landing place of the first settlers"**.

### Special words

Sometimes you use the marks to give special attention to words. In this example a word is being explained.

Frogs' eggs, called **"spawn"**, float on water.

### Single quotation marks (' ')

Some publishers use single quotation marks.

**'Where are you?'** asked Dad.

Frogs' eggs, called **'spawn'**, float on water.

# racist language

Some words are invented and used by people who think badly of other cultures. Language like this, and the people who use it, are called 'racist'.

Examples of these words are:
*boong*, *darkie*, *frog*, *wog*

Racist language is insulting, rude and hurtful. Careful writers and speakers do not use racist language.

**rain** See confusing words: rain, reign, rein.

**raw** See **confusing words**: raw, roar.

**read** See **confusing words**: read, red, reed.

# reading

Reading is an important part of being a writer. Most writers read a lot.

Here are some of the reasons writers read a lot:
• It helps them to grow their vocabulary
• It helps them to understand different styles of writing
• News events can give them ideas for stories
• They research ideas and information for their books

**real** See **confusing words**: real, really and real, reel.

**really** See **confusing words**: real, really.

# recount

A recount text is writing that is about things that have already happened, such as past experiences or events.

**Nonfiction**

Recounts can be about true events. Some different types of nonfiction recounts are:

- **anecdote** (a short story about an event or experience the writer or speaker remembers from the past) See anecdote.
- **autobiography** (a person's writing about the story of his or her own life) See autobiography.
- **diary** (a very personal style of writing where a writer records private thoughts and events in his or her life) See diary.
- **journal** (a writer's records of events or experiences at the time they happen. A journal is often used by travellers and scientists.) See journal.
- **letter writing** (In personal letters, the writer often recounts what has been happening in his or her life.) See letter writing.
- **news story** (a journalist's record of an event that has happened lately) See journalism.

**Fiction**

Recounts can be about imaginary events. Some different types of fiction recounts are:

- **anecdote** (a short story about an imaginary experience told by a storyteller. Tall tales are an example. They recount either funny or unbelievable stories.) See humour.
- **diary** (a diary style telling of events experienced by an imaginary character. An example is *Penny Pollard's Diary* by Robin Klein.) See diary.

**Notes on style**

Remember these points when you write a recount:

- **when, where, who, what** (Recounts mention when and where something happened, what happened and who was involved.)

- **tense** (Because recounts are about things that have already happened, the verbs are mainly in the past tense.) See **tense**.

- **first person** (Diaries, journals, autobiographies and letter writing are often about the writer, so pronouns like *I*, *me*, *my*, *mine*, *we*, *us* and *ours* are used.)

- **order** (The events in recounts are usually written in chronological order — the order that they happened in time.) See **order**.

**red** See **confusing words**: read, red, reed.

**reed** See **confusing words**: read, red, reed.

**reel** See **confusing words**: real, reel.

# reference texts

Reference texts are used for researching ideas and information and for editing your writing.

### Researching information

Useful reference books for researching information are:
- An **encyclopedia** (The information is usually under headwords in alphabetical order.)
- An **information report** (The information is usually under headings in chapters.)

### Editing your writing

The main reference texts for writing and editing are:
- A **dictionary** for checking spelling, word meanings, grammar (parts of speech) and pronunciations
- A **thesaurus** for synonyms and antonyms
- A **style guide** for checking abbreviations, capital letters, confusing words, grammar, punctuation, style and text types. It also gives hints on techniques writers use. The *Junior Writers Guide* is a style guide.

# reflective writing

Reflective writing is a very personal form of writing. The author thinks about feelings and experiences in the past and what those experiences mean now or in the future.

Reflective writing is often in personal diaries, journals, poetry and personal letters between friends.

To find more detail on text types for reflective writing, see diary, journal and letter writing.

**reign** See **confusing words**: rain, reign, rein.

**rein** See **confusing words**: rain, reign, rein.

# report

A report gives facts about a topic. The topic may be one subject (for example, *bees*) or a group of things (for example, *insects*). The facts are organised so they are easy for the reader to find and understand.

Reports often have three main parts:

- an **introduction** to tell readers the topic and describe what the report will focus on about the topic
- **detailed facts** organised under headings and in paragraphs (It can also have diagrams, photographs, maps and charts with labels and captions.)
- a **summary** of what the facts say about the topic

To write a report an author usually needs to:

- **Research information** (Check books, search the Internet, do interviews and take notes. See note-taking.)
- **Choose information** (Select the information that is most suitable for the focus of the report.)
- **Organise information** (Decide on the main headings for the report. This often becomes the 'Table of Contents'. Group the information under these headings.)
- **Write a draft** (Use the information in your research notes to write paragraphs under the main headings.)
- **Check your draft** (Make sure your paragraphs focus on the topic of each heading.)

For hints on planning, drafting and revising your writing, see writing process.

(Turn the page for an example of a report. →)

## THE GIANT SNAKE

**Introduction**

All snakes are legless reptiles. They come from a lizard ancestor about 80 million years ago. Some snakes are venomous, but many are not. This report is about a non-venomous snake, the giant anaconda.

**Habitat**

The giant anaconda lives in South America near river water, and sometimes it climbs trees. Its habitat is being taken over by humans.

**Appearance**

The anaconda grows to about 7.5 metres long. One of the longest snakes in the world, it is dark green with big, black spots.

**Food**

The anaconda waits in water at night for animals that come to drink. It is a python, so it does not poison its prey. It pounces on animals when they drink. Prey as big as a young pig is squeezed to death and then eaten.

**Summary**

If the anaconda's habitat is destroyed, the snake will become extinct. This snake plays an important part in the environment. Humans are its main enemy.

**Notes on style:**

Many reports follow these writing techniques:

- **Verbs** are in the general present tense.
  All snakes **are** legless reptiles. They **do not have** eyelids. They **hunt** prey.

- Use the **impersonal** pronoun *it* to write about animals.
  A snake can move by using the scales on **its** belly.

- **Go from general facts to details**. Start with words like *all*, *every*, *many* and *most* and then move to words like *some*, *few* and *only one*.
  **All** snakes are reptiles. **Some** snakes are venomous.

# research

Research is a part of the writing process. It is when authors find the information they need for a writing project. Research includes interviewing, reading, note-taking and experimenting with ideas and methods (for example, testing recipes).

Research is done by writers for both fiction and nonfiction writing. Fiction writers do research about places for their settings and people or animals they want to use as characters. Nonfiction writers find detailed information about their topic so their writing is accurate.

Some of the research methods are:

- **library research** (background reading of encyclopedias, information reports, newspapers, etc)
- **Internet research** (websites — check whether you can trust the information)
- **interviews** (experts on the topic, witnesses)
- **experiments** (testing processes, recipes or activities to check that they work)

For more information and ideas, see note-taking, reference texts, report and writing process.

**response text** See review.

# review

A review is writing in which the author gives a professional opinion about an event or product. Reviews can be about books, music, plays or films. They are sometimes called *critical reviews* or *response texts*.

A book review often has three main parts:
- **introduction** (background about the book — author, illustrator, publisher and price, enough story details so the reader will understand the review, but not enough information to give away how the story ends)
- **opinion of contents** (some details about what the reviewer liked or didn't like about the book — comments about characters, setting, plot and style of the writing)
- **summary** (a recommendation — who is the book suitable for?)

Here is an example.

---

### ALEX AND THE GLASS SLIPPER

Written and illustrated by Amanda Graham
Published by Era Publications (1992)
Paperback $14.95

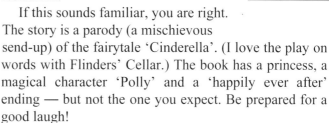

Alex is an overworked and underpaid cook at the Flinders' Cellar Restaurant. His bosses treat him badly and use his cake to enter a royal baking contest, while Alex must work at the restaurant.

If this sounds familiar, you are right. The story is a parody (a mischievous send-up) of the fairytale 'Cinderella'. (I love the play on words with Flinders' Cellar.) The book has a princess, a magical character 'Polly' and a 'happily ever after' ending — but not the one you expect. Be prepared for a good laugh!

This book is suitable for children ages 7-12. Highly recommended for school libraries and the home.

---

See also humour and parody.

# revising

Revising is part of the writing process. After writing a rough draft, an author needs to revise the work to get it ready for editors to read.

### Finding the problems

Here are some methods writers use to revise and improve their writing:

- Read your draft to yourself several times. If something is not right, it will annoy you.
- Put your draft away and read it again the next day (or even later). This helps you to think more clearly about whether your writing makes sense.
- Read your draft out loud. If your sentences are clumsy, you will find them hard to read.

### Fixing the problems

There are three things you can do to fix any problem you find in your draft. You can do them on paper, but it is easier and quicker to do them on a word processor.

- **Add** words, sentences or paragraphs. This is important if you find some information is missing.
- **Delete** words, sentences or paragraphs. Sometimes you will discover that you have repeated information or written things that are unnecessary.
- **Shift** words, sentences or paragraphs. Sometimes you will find that you have words or ideas out of order.

To find out about the next stages in writing, see editing, proofreading and writing process.

# rhetorical questions

Rhetorical (/re-**tor**-rik-ul/) questions are questions to which the speaker or writer does not want an answer.

I ate ten pies. **Can you imagine that?** Ten pies!

# rhyme

Rhyme is words that have the same or similar end sounds. The following sets of words rhyme.

you — two — few — blue — do
chair — stare — pear — where — their

**Notes on style:**
- Rhyming words can end with the same letters (*rain — train*), but often they do not (*lane — main*).
- Rhyming words do not always have the same number of syllables (*see — agree — happily*).
- Poets usually use rhyming words at the ends of lines. This example has an AA pattern — line 1 rhymes with line 2.

> Rhyming can be fun to **do**,
> Especially when words come to **you**.

The following example has an AABB pattern. The rhyme *never — clever* in line 3 is called an *internal rhyme*.

> Rhyming can be fun to **do**,
> Especially when words come to **you**.
> But it's **never** so **clever** to write all **day**,
> When you cannot think of a thing to **say**!

Here is an ABAB rhyming pattern.

> Rhyming can be fun to **do**,
> When words come to your **head**.
> But when the words won't come to **you**,
> Do something else **instead**!

**rhyming couplet** See couplet.

190

# rhythm

Rhythm is the pattern of strong and weak beats that sounds make in words or music.

## Poetry and verse

Listen to the **1**, 2 — **1**, 2 pattern of strong and weak beats as you read the words in these two lines of verse.

> **Clap** your **hands** and **stamp** your **feet**,
> **Slap** your **side** and **feel** the **beat**.

Compare that rhythm to the pattern in the following lines. Listen for the **1**, 2, 3 — **1**, 2, 3 pattern.

> **Ro**ses smell **pret**ty, their **pet**als do **tick**le,
> But **watch** for the **stem** or you'll **sure** get a **prick**le.

## Prose

Rhythm is important in prose writing. Good rhythm makes words flow more smoothly. It also makes them easier to read. Here is an example of an opening paragraph to a story.

> Long, long ago when the world was young and dinosaurs ruled the land, an egg in a wide round nest split open. Out popped a tiny animal. It looked about and then scampered away to hide among leafy ferns.

The following paragraph might begin the same story, but it is harder to read because the rhythm is not so smooth.

> Once, dinosaurs ruled the world. One day, in a wide round nest an egg split open. A small animal came out. It looked around. Then it ran into some leafy ferns and hid.

a
b
c
d
e
f
g
h
i
j
k
l
m
n
o
p
q
r
s
t
u
v
w
x
y
z

**right** See **confusing words**: right, write.

**road** See **confusing words**: road, rode.

**roar** See **confusing words**: raw, roar.

**rode** See **confusing words**: road, rode.

**root** See **confusing words**: root, route.

# root words

There are three main parts to words — roots, prefixes and suffixes. A root word is the main or basic part of any word.

Some roots words are:
  true, plant, write

Prefixes can be added to the beginning of many root words to make new words and meanings.
  **un**true, **trans**plant, **re**write

Suffixes can be added to the end of many root words.
  tru**ly**, plant**ing**, writ**ers**

Sometimes, two root words can be joined to make a compound word.
  some + one = someone; rain + bow = rainbow

Root words can stand by themselves.
  happy, easy

Prefixes and suffixes do not make sense by themselves.
  un-, -ness, -ly

For more information on how to build words, see compound words, prefixes and suffixes.

**route** See **confusing words**: root, route.

**rung** See **confusing words**: rung, wrung.

# saga

*Saga* is a very old word from Iceland. It used to mean 'what is told'. Sagas in Iceland were long tales of heroes, kings and their families. At first, they were spoken stories passed on by storytellers. After many years, the stories were written down.

Today, we think of a saga as a long story about a family.

**sail** See **confusing words**: sail, sale.

**sale** See **confusing words**: sail, sale.

# sarcasm

Sarcasm is the use of humour to make a negative comment about someone or something. It is often used by critics — people who write reviews of books, films, plays and other things such as restaurants.

Reviewers sometimes use sarcasm to make their review more entertaining, but it can be hurtful to people in the review. Here are some sarcastic sentences a reviewer might use about a restaurant or a book.

> The steak would have been wonderful — **if I could have cut it!**

> The book is good for **bedtime reading — so boring it sends you to sleep straightaway!**

To find out about other ways writers make the audience laugh, see humour.

To find out more about critical writing, see review.

**sauce** See **confusing words**: sauce, source.

**saw** See **confusing words**: saw, soar, sore.

**scent** See **confusing words**: cent, scent, sent.

a
b
c
d
e
f
g
h
i
j
k
l
m
n
o
p
q
r
s
t
u
v
w
x
y
z

# screenplay

A screenplay is a script written for a film or movie. It includes the words the actors say and scenes the camera must take. A screenplay is similar in style to a play script.

To find out more about writing in this style, see dialogue and play script.

**sea** See **confusing words**: sea, see.

**see** See **confusing words**: sea, see.

**sell** See **confusing words**: cell, sell.

# semicolon (;)

The semicolon marks a break in a sentence; it is a stronger pause than a comma. A semicolon *links* ideas; a comma *separates* ideas.

> The rain was heavy; the river was rising.

The semicolon in this sentence links the two ideas about *the rain* and *the river*. It makes the second idea sound more exciting than if it is a separate sentence.

> The rain was heavy. The river was rising.

Semicolons are sometimes used to link the ideas in a list. This usually happens when each item in the list is a sentence.

> People help the environment when:
> • They use their own carry bags when food shopping;
> • They recycle waste plastic, metal and paper;
> • They reduce the waste they make.

**sent** See **confusing words**: cent, scent, sent.

# sentence

A sentence is a group of words that express a complete thought. A sentence has two main parts: it has a *subject* (what the sentence is about) and a *predicate* (what happens to the subject).

> The dog [**subject**] is barking [**predicate**].

There are four things a sentence can express:

- statements (That dog is barking.)
- commands (Stop that dog from barking.)
- questions (Is that dog barking?)
- exclamations (Hey, that dog is barking!)

Look up any of these topics in this guide for more information.

Sentences begin with a capital letter and end with a full stop, question mark, exclamation mark or ellipsis points.

> **S**top your dog from barking**!**
> **W**hich dog**?**
> **T**he dog over there by the**...**
> **B**ut that's not my dog**.**

**serial** See **confusing words**: cereal, serial.

# setting

A setting is the place and time a story happens. A writer often describes the setting of a story at the beginning of the tale. In a play, this is called the *scene*. The setting is important because it makes a difference to how the characters behave and what happens to them.

**Place**

The reader needs to understand the place where the characters live or act out the story. For example, the characters might be:

- Shipwrecked at sea and left on an island
- Travelling across a very hot desert
- Living on a very big farm in the country
- Living in a very small apartment in a big city
- Living in a fantasy world with monsters and elves

**Time**

The reader needs to understand when the story takes place. For example, it might be:

- **In the past** (Historical novels, dinosaur tales, biographies, myths and legends are set in the past. This can make it interesting for the audience to see how people or animals used to live.)
- **In the present** (Modern family stories, dramas, romances and comedies are set in the present, so the audience already understands the setting. This is called a *contemporary* setting.)
- **In the future** (Science-fiction stories are often set in the future. This can make it interesting for the audience to imagine what life might be like in the future.)

To write about a setting so the audience can imagine and picture it, an author uses descriptive writing. To find out some of the ways an author does this, see descriptive writing.

**several** See **confusing words**: couple, few, several.

**sew** See **confusing words**: sew, so, sow.

# sexist language

*Sexist language* means using language in a way that makes either males or females in the audience feel that they have been left out or treated unfairly. Careful writers try to make sure that their language is *non-sexist*.

### Sexist words

Some words are sexist because they are inaccurate or biased towards males or females. The names of jobs can often be like this. For example:

> *fireman* (Do only men fight fires?)

Here are some sexist words (and some non-sexist words you can use in their place).

| *Sexist* | *Non-sexist* |
| --- | --- |
| police**man** | police officer |
| store**man** | storeperson or storeworker |
| waitr**ess** | waiter or server |

### Pronouns

Careful writers make sure that the pronouns they use do not make their writing sexist. Here is an example of writing that is sexist because of the pronouns.

> A soccer player makes sure **he** keeps fit.

The word *he* suggests that only boys or men play soccer. This ignores all the girls and women who play soccer. The sentence can be rewritten to avoid this.

> Soccer **players make sure they** keep fit.
> A soccer player **needs to** keep fit.

### How characters behave

Treating all female or all male characters the same way is called *stereotyping*. If you always have a father character fixing a fence or the car, while the mother cleans the house or cooks, your writing is sexist. There are many men today who do the cooking and women who use tools to fix things. In toy catalogues, you may find 'boy' toys in advertisements showing active boys in bold colours playing with action figures, while advertisements for 'girl' toys have soft colours and girls playing with dolls. Avoid stereotyping in your writing.

**shear** See **confusing words**: shear, sheer.

**sheer** See **confusing words**: shear, sheer.

# shortened words

People often shorten words so they are quicker to say. A shortened word sometimes becomes so common that the original, longer word is forgotten. For example, the word *zoo* is a shortened form of *zoological garden*.

Shortened words are useful because they save time and space. Here are some common shortened words and the words or phrases they came from.

| Shortened word | Original word |
| --- | --- |
| ad | advertisement |
| bus | omnibus |
| fax | facsimile |
| limo | limousine |
| plane | aeroplane |
| vet | veterinary surgeon |

Some writers prefer not to use shortened words in formal writing unless the word is so well known that people no longer use the original form.

198

# short story

A short story is a narrative that does not take long to read. They are popular because they can be very entertaining.

Here are some ways an author keeps a story short:
• The story has very few characters.
• The setting is just one place and one time.
• The problem for the characters is introduced early.
• The characters fix the problem with one main action.
• The exciting climax is often the conclusion.

For examples, see anecdote and fable.

**should** See could, should, would.

**should of** See **confusing words**: could've, could of.

**should've** See **confusing words**: could've, could of.

# sibilance

Sibilance is the repeated use of /s/ sounds to create a special effect in sentences. It is a way authors create word pictures using sounds to remind readers of things or feelings they know. It also gives a reader a way to read a text out loud with more drama.

The /s/ sound can remind people of things like:
• **a snake** (The **s**caly **s**erpent **s**lipped down from it**s** tree and **s**ilently **s**lid in**s**ide their tent.)
• **a whistle or song** (**S**ing a **s**ong of **s**ixpen**ce**...)
• **softness or a whisper** (The bree**z**e **s**ent a **s**igh right by hi**s** cheek**s** and whi**s**pered in hi**s** ear.)

Different letters of the alphabet can make the /s/ sound. Listen for it in these words:
    **s**peak, mi**ss**, fen**ce**, **sc**ene, **c**ircle, fo**x**, free**z**e

For an example of sibilance in a poem, see haiku.

# silent letters

Many words are spelled with letters that have no sound. These letters are called *silent letters*. This can make words hard to spell.

Words with silent letters sometimes follow patterns. To discover the silent letter patterns, it is a good idea to study lists of words with the same silent letter.

**Silent letter *b***

The silent letter *b* comes after the letter *m* at word ends.
• bo**mb**, climb, comb, crumb, lamb, limb, numb, thumb

**Silent letter *c***

The silent letter *c* comes after the letter *s* and before the letters *e* or *i* in these words.
• a**sce**nd, crescent, descend, scene, scent
• di**sci**ple, fascinate, science, scissors

**Silent letter *e***

Notice how the silent letter *e* comes after a consonant at the end of words like these.
• hav**e**, hate, give, hive, sneeze, some, home, cute

**Silent letter *g***

The silent letter *g* comes in four main letter patterns:
• Before the letter *n* at the beginning of a word (**gn**at, gnaw, gnome, gnu)
• Before the letter *n* (si**gn**, reign, designer)
• In the letter group *eigh* (w**eigh**, neighbour, sleigh)
• In the letter group *ght* (li**ght**, daughter, bought, weight)

**Silent letter *h***

In most words with a silent letter *h*, the *h* follows the letters *g*, *r* or *w*.
• **gh**astly, gherkin, ghetto, ghost, ghoul
• **rh**inoceros, rhubarb, rhyme, rhythm
• **wh**ale, wharf, what, wheat, when, where, why, white

Some words begin with the silent letter *h*.
• **h**eir, heirloom, honest, honour, hour

### Silent letter *k*

The silent letter *k* is always followed by the letter *n*.
* **kn**ee, knew, knife, knob, knock, know, knuckle

### Silent letter *l*

The silent letter *l* is followed by the letter *k*.
* cha**lk**, stalk, talk, walk, folk

### Silent letter *n*

The silent letter *n* follows the letter *m* at the end of a word.
* autu**mn**, column, condemn, damn, hymn, solemn

### Silent letter *w*

The silent letter *w* usually comes before the letters *ho* and *r* at the beginning of a word.
* **wh**o, whoever, whole, whom, whose
* **wr**ap, wreck, wrestle, wriggle, write, wrong, wry

Three common words do not follow these patterns for the silent *w*:
* ans**w**er, s**w**ord, t**w**o

The silent *w* in these three words can be explained only by their history. Words like *answer* and *two* have interesting stories. If you want to know about them, see WORD HISTORIES: answer and two.

# simile

A simile is a phrase that often begins with the words *like* or *as*. Writers use similes to compare one thing to another. It is a way of building word pictures and making your writing more descriptive.

> His hair curled **like corkscrews** out of his head.

> The first bowl of soup was **as cold as ice**; the second was **as hot as fire**.

# singular

Singular means 'one'. Nouns, verbs and pronouns have singular forms. The opposite of *singular* is *plural* (more than one).

Here is a sentence with a singular pronoun, noun and verb.

> **His dog is** well-trained.

Here is the same sentence with a plural pronoun, noun and verb.

> **Their dogs are** well-trained.

To find out how to write the plural and singular forms of different nouns, pronouns and verbs, see plural.

# singular words

Some words refer to a single person or thing only. They do not have a plural form. Some singular words are:

> *each*, *any*, *nobody*, *nothing*, *none*, *no one*, *anyone*

In a sentence, these words need a singular verb to agree.

> ✗ **Nothing are** wrong.
> ✓ **Nothing is** wrong.

To find out more about making words agree in a sentence, see agreement.

# slang

Slang is the language we use every day in informal speech. It is not usually used in formal writing.

Sometimes slang is useful for dialogue in a story. It can make characters in a story sound real because it is how people often speak.

> "Why are the **cops** next door?" asked Jim.
> "I think the guy has been **nicking** things," said Sam.

If you want to know more, see dialogue, formal/informal writing and swear words.

# slash mark (/)

The slash is a punctuation mark that has different uses. Here are four ways in which it is used.

- **abbreviations** (**c/o** or **c/-** meaning 'care of'; **a/c** meaning 'airconditioner' or 'account')
- **dates** (**5/3/08** or **5/3/2008**)
- **meaning 'or' in word choices** (A person can have red **and/or** blue if **he/she** wishes.)
- **meaning 'per' in measures** (**km/h** means 'kilometres per hour'.)

**so** See **confusing words**: sew, so, sow.

**soar** See **confusing words**: saw, soar, sore.

**son** See **confusing words**: son, sun.

**sore** See **confusing words**: saw, soar, sore.

**source** See **confusing words**: sauce, source.

**sow** See **confusing words**: sew, so, sow.

# speech

Putting speech into writing brings characters to life. There are different ways writers can do this.

- **Callouts** are used for cartoons and comics. Callouts are also called *speech bubbles* or *speech balloons*.
- **Play scripts** are used for speech in a play. The writer lists the characters' names next to words they speak.
- **Quotation marks** are used for words spoken by characters in a story. They are also called *speech marks*.
- **Transcripts** are like play scripts but with real conversations. You would use this method to record an interview with someone.

For examples and more information about speech in writing, see dialogue, direct speech, play script and quotation marks (" ").

**speech bubbles** See callout, dialogue and speech.

**speech marks** See quotation marks (" ").

# spelling

English words have about forty-six different sounds. But there are only twenty-six letters in the alphabet. There are not enough letters to make each sound with just one letter. Some letters and letter groups can have more than one sound. For example:

**a** (cat, wash, water, spa)
**oo** (room, book, fool, flood, brooch)

There are several ways to remember how to spell words. Most of these ways involve remembering words in groups with certain patterns of letters, sounds and meaning. Here are some ways you can remember words or check your spelling.

### Adding endings
Many spelling problems happen when writers add endings to words. Here are some examples.

• **Words ending with -e**
With most words ending with -e, you drop the e when you add suffixes beginning with a vowel.
*-ing*: hope - hoping      leave - leaving
*-al*: nature - natural
*-able*: cure - curable    note - notable

• **Words ending with -ic**
With most words ending with -ic, you add k when you add -ed, -er or -ing.
*picnic*: picnicked, picnicker, picnicking

• **Words ending with -ie**
With most words ending with -ie, you change the ie to y when you add -ing.
die - dying        lie - lying        tie - tying

### • Words ending with *-y*

With most words ending with *-y*, you change the *y* to *i* when you add *-ed*, *-er*, *-es*, *-est* or *-ly*.

> *baby*: babies
> *easy*: easier, easiest, easily
> *carry*: carried, carries, carrier

### • Words ending with a vowel-consonant

With most words ending with a vowel-consonant, you double the consonant when you add *-ed*, *-er* or *-ing*.

> *hop*: hopped, hopper, hopping
> *swim*: swimmer, swimming

## Compound words

Some words are made by joining smaller words. Examples are:

> *butterfly*, *football*, *twenty-five*

To find out more, see compound words.

## More than one spelling for a word

Many words can be spelled in more than one way. Often this is because there are two main forms of English spelling in the world — US and UK English. Some examples are:

### • *-elling* or *-eling*?

Doubling the letter *l* (*modelling*) is usually UK spelling. Not doubling the letter *l* (*modeling*) is usually US spelling.

> (UK spelling) *travelling*, *travelled*, *traveller*
> (US spelling) *traveling*, *traveled*, *traveler*

### • *-ise* or *-ize*?

If you use *-ise*:

> Examples: *finalise*, *itemise*, *memorise*, *realise*
> Exception (the only one): *capsize*

If you use *-ize*:

> Examples: *finalize*, *itemize*, *memorize*, *realize*
> Exceptions: *advise*, *exercise*, *revise*, *surprise* (and many more)

*-ise* is easier to remember because there is only one exception. *-ize* has many exceptions to remember.

(Turn the page for more about spelling. →)

a
b
c
d
e
f
g
h
i
j
k
l
m
n
o
p
q
r
**s**
t
u
v
w
x
y
z

- *-logue* or *-log*?

*-logue* is usually UK spelling. *-log* is usually US spelling.

(UK) *catalogue, dialogue, epilogue*

(US) *catalog, epilog*

- *-our* or *-or*?

*-our* is usually UK spelling. *-or* is usually US spelling.

(UK) *colour, odour, favourite*

(US) *color, odor, favorite*

- *-re* or *-er*?

*-re* on the end of a word is usually UK spelling. *-er* is usually US spelling.

(UK) *centre, theatre, sabre*

(US) *center, theater, saber*

**Plurals**

Many spelling errors are made when people write the plural of words. This is because there are so many ways to spell a plural in English. See plural to find the spelling rules for the plural of these main groups:

- Words that end with **ff** or **fe**
- Words that end with **ful**
- Words that end with **us**
- Words that end with **o**
- Words that end with **s, x, z, ch, sh** or **ss**
- Words that end with **y**

**Rules**

Some word groups follow spelling patterns or rules, but there are usually some exceptions to the rule. Here are some of these spelling patterns:

- **consonant-vowel-consonant + e**

Adding an *e* to the end of a consonant-vowel-consonant word changes the vowel from a short to a long sound.

Examples are: *cap/cape, bit/bite, hop/hope*

To find more examples, look up -e.

- ***i* before *e* except after *c***
  *i* comes before *e*, except after *c*, in words with an /ee/ sound.
  Examples are: *belief, siege, ceiling, deceive, receive*
  Exceptions are: *protein, seize*

## Same sound, different spelling
Many words sound the same but have different spellings and different meanings. Some examples are:
  *to, too, two; hear, here; hoarse, horse; knew, new*

To find other words like these, see **confusing words**.

## Same spelling, different sound
Some words look the same but have more than one sound and meaning. Some examples are:
  *bow, row, tear, read, lead, wind, wound*

To find out about words like these, see **homographs**.

## Silent letters
Many words have letters that are not sounded. Some examples are:
  *la**b**, **s**cissors, hym**n**, **k**not, **w**hat, **w**hole*

To find out about other silent letters, see **silent letters**.

## Troublesome words
These words are from a list of 'troublesome' words that people find hard to spell. Practise spelling these words until you can remember them.
  *adviser, benefited, broccoli, cemetery, certainly, changeable, chimney, conscience, conscious, coolly, curtain, definitely, desperate, development, embarrass, exceed, existence, February, forfeit, forty, gauge, harass, independent, insistent, irritable, knowledgeable, leisure, librarian, mischievous, mysterious, ninth, occasion, preferred, pursue, pursuit, receive, recommend, repetition, seize, separate, similar, sincerely, suffered, truly, unnecessary, Wednesday, weird*

(Turn the page for more about spelling. →)

a
b
c
d
e
f
g
h
i
j
k
l
m
n
o
p
q
r
s
t
u
v
w
x
y
z

### Syllables
It can be helpful to break long words into syllables.
> unnecessary (un-nec-es-sar-y)

To find out more about this, see syllable.

### Word parts
Many words are made of three different types of word parts. They are *prefixes*, *root words* and *suffixes*. Some words are easier to spell if you remember these parts.
> *read* (root word): reads, reading, reader, readable, readability, unreadable, reread

To find out more about word parts, see plural, prefixes, root words and suffixes.

**stair** See **confusing words**: stair, stare.

**stake** See **confusing words**: stake, steak.

**stalk** See **confusing words**: stalk, stork.

**stanza** See verse.

**stare** See **confusing words**: stair, stare.

# statements

Statements are sentences that state or declare something. They are the most commonly used sentence type in most writing. They do not ask questions, give instructions or exclaim anything. Statements usually begin with a capital letter and end with a full stop.

> Bees gather pollen from flowers.
> The storm damaged many houses.
> The weather tomorrow will be windy and wet.

See also sentence.

**steak** See **confusing words**: stake, steak.

**steal** See **confusing words**: steal, steel.

**steel** See **confusing words**: steal, steel.

**storey** See **confusing words**: storey, story.

**stork** See **confusing words**: stalk, stork.

**story** See **confusing words**: storey, story.

# storyboard

A storyboard is something writers do at the planning stage of a writing project before they do a first draft. It is a way some authors map out and organise their ideas.

In fiction writing, storyboards are often notes in a chart. The chart reminds the writer of the ideas and their order in the beginning, middle and end of a story. It also helps a writer to see where some ideas don't make sense in a story and need to be moved or deleted.

For a picture book, many illustrators draw small sketches called *thumbnails* before they begin the real drawings. The thumbnails show the main idea for each page in the book.

In nonfiction, the *table of contents* of a book is a kind of storyboard. After doing the research, a writer lists the main ideas as headings in an order that makes sense.The headings show the writer whether any important information has been left out or whether ideas are under the right heading.

# style

*Style* is the way writers express themselves. Different writers have their own special way of saying things.

People often mix up *grammar* and *style*. Grammar is about how words are organised to make meaning; style is about the choice of words used and the sounds of the writing. The following sentences mean the same but say it in different styles.

- **Formal style**: Heavy rain fell today.
- **Informal style**: It rained cats and dogs today.
- **Personal style**: It rained a lot today and I got wet.
- **Poetic style**: Rain, rain, it rained all day; I wish that it would go away.

For more about style, see formal/informal writing.

# subject

There are two main parts to a sentence — the *subject* and the *predicate*. The subject is the person or thing that the sentence is about. It is the topic of a sentence.

**The frog** spends its life in or near water.

This sentence is about *the frog*. So *the frog* is the subject of the sentence. The rest of the sentence is called the 'predicate' (what is said about the frog).

For more information, see predicate and sentence.

The subject can be made up of several words and phrases. It can also be in different places in a sentence.

**Most frogs and toads** live near water.

**The frog, being an amphibian,** lives near water.

Throughout the year, **frogs** live near water.

Do **frogs** live near water throughout the year?

The subject must agree with its verb. A singular subject must have a singular verb. A plural subject needs a plural verb.

✗ **A frog live** near water.

✓ **A frog lives** near water.

✓ **Frogs live** near water.

For more information, see agreement.

# suffixes

Suffixes are word endings. We use suffixes to change words into different parts of speech.

**Suffixes that change words into adjectives**
- -**able**: agreeable, enjoyable, suitable, valuable
- -**al**: coastal, comical, musical, natural, practical
- -**ive**: active, creative, exclusive, expensive, positive
- -**ful**: beautiful, cheerful, dreadful, graceful, useful
- -**ous**: adventurous, curious, famous, furious
- -**y**: cuddly, easy, healthy, prickly, shiny, skinny

**Suffixes that change words into nouns**
- -**ance**: allowance, appearance, distance, entrance
- -**dom**: boredom, freedom, kingdom, stardom
- -**ence**: confidence, difference, experience, patience
- -**ment**: government, management, movement
- -**ness**: business, foolishness, happiness, kindness
- -**th**: health, length, strength, width
- -**tion**: infection, pollution, protection, solution

**Suffixes that change words into adverbs**
- -**ly**: easily, hopefully, quickly, sadly, slowly

**Suffixes that are used to compare**
We use suffixes to make adjectives and adverbs that compare two or more things.
- -**er**: (adjective) bigger (adverb) further
- -**est**: (adjective) biggest (adverb) furthest

**Suffixes that form plurals**
You can find out about this topic under plural.

**Suffixes for verb tenses**
The suffixes -*s*, -*ed* and -*ing* are used to form the present and past tenses of most verbs.

helps, helped, helping

# summary

A summary is a short description of the most important ideas and information in a piece of writing. A summary does not give all the detail. It just notes the main points.

**sun** See **confusing words**: son, sun.

# swear words

Swear words are words that some people use when they are angry or excited. It is better not to use swear words in your writing because many people find them upsetting or rude.

# syllable

A syllable is a single unit of pronunciation in a word. There is always one vowel sound in a syllable. A word can have one or more than one syllable.

*for* has one syllable.

*fortune* has two syllables (for-tune).

*fortunate* has three syllables (for-tun-ate).

*fortunately* has four syllables (for-tun-ate-ly).

*unfortunately* has five syllables (un-for-tun-ate-ly).

A syllable can have one letter or several letters. Each of the following words has only one syllable. The shortest has one letter. The longest has nine letters.

*a, or, for, poor, floor, floors, brought, screened, squelched*

Breaking a long word into syllables can help you spell it.

*un - for - tun - ate - ly*

Poets often choose a word because it has the right number of beats (syllables) for a poem. See rhythm.

# symbols

Symbols are marks used in place of words. They are like abbreviations because they are short ways of writing words. Here are some examples.

### Ampersand (&)

The ampersand, &, is a symbol for the word *and*. It is used in addresses, company names, signs and book titles. It is not used in formal writing.

> *Deadly* **&** *Dangerous Snakes* by Ted Mertens

### Copyright (©)

The copyright symbol, ©, shows who owns the copyright to a text or a picture. You can write this on any writing that is your own work.

> Text © Pedro Almaro, 2002

You cannot copy someone else's writing without permission. See plagiarism to find out about this.

### Money ($, ¢, €, £, d)

Symbols are used for money all over the world. They are only used with numerals.

> ✗ five $
> ✓ $5

If you want to know where the symbol $ came from, look up WORD HISTORIES: dollar symbol ($).

### Per cent (%)

The words *per cent* mean 'per hundred'. The symbol % is used only with numerals.

> ✗ five %
> ✓ 5%
> ✓ five percent

**symbols** See **confusing words**: cymbals, symbols.

# synonyms

Synonyms are words that are the same or similar in meaning.

> **small** — little, tiny, narrow, light, short
> **big** — large, huge, enormous, fat, wide, tall, heavy

Good writers use synonyms to avoid using the same word more than once in a sentence or paragraph.

Writers and editors use a thesaurus to find synonyms. Modern word-processing programs on computers have a thesaurus.

Writers also find words that are opposite in meaning very useful. These are in a thesaurus too. If you want to find out about these words, see antonyms.

**tail** See **confusing words**: tail, tale.

**take** See **confusing words**: bring, take.

**tale** See **confusing words**: tail, tale.

**teach** See **confusing words**: learn, teach.

# tense

*Tense* in writing means '*when* something happened'. There are three main tenses — past, present and future. These tenses are shown by the way you write verbs. With most verbs you change the endings.

- **Present tense** (is happening now or all the time)
  *shout, shouts, is shouting, are shouting*
- **Past tense** (has already happened)
  *shouted, was shouting, were shouting*
- **Future tense** (has not yet happened)
  *will shout, shall shout, will be shouting*

The endings used for most verbs are -**s**, -**ed** and -**ing**. There is a large group of verbs that do not use -*ed* for the past tense. These are called *irregular verbs*. To find out about these verbs, see **verbs**: Irregular verbs.

# text messaging

Text messaging means sending short text messages by a mobile telephone or pager. It is also called *Short Message Service (SMS)*. People use very short forms of words in text messages, sometimes by using numerals and letters that sound like words. For example:

**CU L8R** means 'See you later'.

# text types

Writers create different kinds of texts for different purposes. These different kinds of texts are called *text types*. They are also called *genres*.

Authors change their writing to suit different text types. The ways their writing might change include:
- the **order** and **organisation** of the ideas in the writing
- the **style** of the writing (poetry, prose, formal, informal)
- the **grammar** (sentence types, verbs, pronouns, etc)
You can find out more by looking up these headings.

Fiction, nonfiction and poetry all have different text types. You can find examples and details about each of these text types under these headings:

- argument (to give an opinion or persuade someone to do something)
- discussion (to compare opinions on a topic)
- explanation (to explain how something works)
- narrative (to tell a story)
- poetry (to express ideas, thoughts and stories in a memorable way through word pictures and sounds)
- procedural text (to explain how to do something)
- recount (to tell about something that has happened)
- report (to give facts about a topic)
- review (to give an opinion on what is good or bad about a book, film, play, music or service)

**the** See a, the and articles.

**their** See **confusing words**: their, there, they're.

**them** See **confusing words**: them, those.

# theme

A theme is the main idea a piece of writing is about.

- In a **fable** or a **parable**, the theme is the moral. It is the lesson that the storyteller wants to give to the audience.
- In a **report**, the introduction and the summary describe the writer's theme; the focus of the report.
- In a **haiku**, the last line expresses its theme. It is the main idea behind the word picture the poet creates.

To find more detail on theme, see narrative.

**there** See **confusing words**: their, there, they're.

**they're** See **confusing words**: their, there, they're.

**those** See **confusing words**: them, those.

# time

There are many ways you can write the time. Using words can be a very long way of writing the time.

fifty-five minutes after the eleventh hour in the day

Here are some other ways you could write the time:
fifty-five minutes past eleven in the morning
five minutes before noon
5 to 12 midday
11.55 am (or 11.55 a.m. or 11.55 A.M.)
11.55 in the morning

You write the time most often in diaries, journals, letter writing, notes and recounts. To find out more, see abbreviations.

**tire** See **confusing words**: tire, tyre.

# titles

Titles can refer to people (Mr, Mrs, Ms, Miss, Dr, Capt) or creative works (books, paintings, plays, poems, songs, stories).

### Titles of people

There are several different titles that can be given to people. The titles tell you something about them. Titles are usually abbreviated when they are used with a person's name. Here are some examples:

Capt or Cpt (a captain of a ship, plane or team, or a military officer)
Dr (doctor)
Miss (a girl or unmarried woman)
Mr (a man)
Mrs (a married woman)
Ms (a woman)

For more information about writing titles of people, see **abbreviations** and **capital letters**: Proper nouns.

### Titles of creative works

The main words in the titles of books, paintings, plays, poems, songs and stories begin with a capital letter.

**Y**oung **W**riters **G**uide
**M**ona **L**isa
**P**hantom of the **O**pera
**W**innie the **P**ooh

You can find more information and examples if you look up **capital letters**: Titles of creative works.

**to** See prepositions.

**to** See **confusing words**: to, too, two.

**toe** See **confusing words**: toe, tow.

# tone

Tone is the writer's feelings and attitude when writing to an audience. It is part of a writer's style.

When you write, the tone you use will show whether you are angry or happy, personal or impersonal, polite or rude. You do this by the words and sentences you choose. Here are some examples.

- **Angry, demanding, impersonal**
  Fix it right away!
- **Polite, patient, formal**
  Please fix it as soon as possible.
- **Personal, friendly, informal**
  I'd be really happy if you could fix it for me soon.

To find out about writing styles to create a certain tone in your writing, see formal/informal writing, impersonal writing and personal writing.

**too** See **confusing words**: to, too, two.

# topic sentence

A topic sentence is usually the first sentence of a paragraph or a piece of writing. It gives the reader the subject or main idea of the paragraph or writing.

In this example, the topic sentence tells you what the paragraph is about. The other sentences give details.

> **The eagle is a bird of prey.** It hunts and eats other animals. Eagles eat fish, small mammals, reptiles and other birds.

The introduction to a small nonfiction book can begin with a topic sentence. It tells the reader which parts of a topic the writing will cover.

> This book is about flamingos — where they live and breed, and how they feed and survive in the wild.

From this topic sentence the reader knows that the book will *not* be about zoos or the flamingo's history.

For more about topic sentences, see paragraphs.

218

**tow** See **confusing words**: toe, tow.

# traditional literature

Each culture in the world has its own collection of tales, songs and poems that have been passed on by parents, grandparents and storytellers. This collection is the traditional literature of that culture.

Traditional literature belongs to the people or 'folk'. This is where we get the word *folktale*. It is free of copyright because the writers are no longer known, or died so long ago that anyone can now retell the stories.

It is not plagiarism to retell a traditional tale in your own words. It is plagiarism only if you copy the words someone else used to retell the story. For more information about this, see plagiarism.

Many types of traditional literature are described in this *Junior Writers Guide*. If you want to know more about them, see ballad, fable, fairytale, folktale, legend, literature, lyric, myth, parable, plays and saga.

**two** See **confusing words**: to, too, two and WORD HISTORIES: two.

**tyre** See **confusing words**: tire, tyre.

**units of measure** See measures.

# usage

Usage means the ways in which words are used in writing and speech. Careful writers make good word choices so the meaning is clear. To find words that cause writers problems, look up confusing words.

**vain** See **confusing words**: vain, vein.

**vein** See **confusing words**: vain, vein.

# verbs

A verb is a word or a word group that shows what the subject of a sentence is *doing*, *being*, *saying* or *thinking*. Every sentence must have a verb.

"The lion **escaped**," **shouted** the zookeeper.
In this sentence, the verb *escaped* shows what the lion *did*; the verb *shouted* shows what the zookeeper *said*.

**Types of verbs**
Different types of verbs suit the jobs writers need them to do in sentences.

• **action verbs** (*walk*, *run*, *jump*, *hold*, *eat*, *put*, *mix*)
Action verbs are very useful in procedural texts, recounts, explanations and narratives.
**Add** milk and butter, then **heat** and **stir** the sauce.

• **speech verbs** (*say*, *whisper*, *call*, *cry*, *ask*, *tell*, *reply*)
Speech verbs are very important when you write dialogue. They are also used a lot in news articles.
"**Speak** to me," **called** the rescue worker.

• **thinking verbs** (*think*, *know*, *believe*, *wish*, *want*, *love*, *enjoy*, *like*, *understand*, *feel*, *imagine*, *wonder*)
Thinking verbs are useful for describing characters. They show how characters think and feel.
Anna **wondered** about Sophie and **hoped** she was safe.

• **linking verbs** (*is*, *am*, *are*, *has*, *have*, *do*, *does*, *seem*, *means*, *looks* (like), *tastes*, *smells*, *sounds*)
Linking verbs link the subject of a sentence to words that give more information about it. They are used a lot in information reports.
There **is** a fly in my soup. It **tastes** awful. I **am** angry.

• **helper verbs** (*is*, *am*, *are*, *was*, *were*, *been*, *has*, *have*, *had*, *will*, *would*, *should*, *could*, *might*)
Helper verbs are used to build verbs groups that tell when something happened. We use them to form different verb tenses.
I **have worked** for hours. I **will stop** soon.

## Forms of verbs

Verbs have different forms that let writers express different meanings. Most verb forms follow patterns.

- **singular and plural** (*walks - walk*, *says - say*, *thinks - think*, *is - are*, *has - have*)

Verbs have singular and plural forms. We use this to make them agree with the subject of a sentence.

> **Matt likes** to run, but the other **kids like** to walk.

The verb *likes* is singular to agree with the subject *Matt*. The verb *like* is plural to agree with the subject *kids*. To find out more about this, see **plural**: Plural verbs and singular.

- **tenses** (*hops*, *is hopping*, *hopped*, *will hop*)

Verbs have tenses so writers can tell when something happened. There are three main tenses — past, present and future. Here are some examples.

> *Present tense* (actions happening now)
> Clouds **cover** the sky.
> Clouds **are covering** the sky.

The present tense is used a lot in information reports.

> *Past tense* (actions have already happened)
> Clouds **covered** the sky.
> Clouds **were covering** the sky.

The past tense is used a lot in recounts and narratives.

> *Future tense* (actions have not yet happened)
> Clouds **will cover** the sky.
> Clouds **are going to cover** the sky.

The future tense is used a lot in information reports and arguments.

> If we do not change our ways, we **will be** sorry.

- **participles** (*hopped*, *hopping*)

Participles are verb forms that are used to make other forms of verbs. To find out about them, see participles.

(Turn the page for more about verbs. →)

a
b
c
d
e
f
g
h
i
j
k
l
m
n
o
p
q
r
s
t
u
v
w
x
y
z

a
b
c
d
e
f
g
h
i
j
k
l
m
n
o
p
q
r
s
t
u
v
w
x
y
z

**Irregular verbs**

You can form the past tense and past participle of most verbs by adding the ending -d or -ed. These are called *regular verbs*.

The frog **hopped**. It **had hopped** out of the pond.

Verbs that do not follow this rule are called *irregular verbs*. The verb *run* is an irregular verb.

The rabbit **ran**. It **had run** into its burrow.

Irregular verbs are a problem to people learning the English language. Here is a list of some irregular verbs.

| Present | Past; past participle | Present | Past; past participle |
|---------|----------------------|---------|----------------------|
| am | was; have been | drive | drove; has driven |
| are | were; has been | eat | ate; has eaten |
| bear | bore; has borne | fall | fell; has fallen |
| beat | beat; has beaten | feed | fed; has fed |
| become | became; has become | feel | felt; has felt |
| begin | began; has begun | fight | fought; has fought |
| bind | bound; has bound | find | found; has found |
| bite | bit; has bitten | fling | flung; has flung |
| bleed | bled; had bled | fly | flew; has flown |
| blow | blew; has blown | forget | forgot; has forgotten |
| break | broke; has broken | forgive | forgave; has forgiven |
| breed | bred; has bred | freeze | froze; has frozen |
| bring | brought; has brought | get | got; has got |
| build | built; has built | give | gave; has given |
| buy | bought; has bought | grind | ground; has ground |
| catch | caught; has caught | grow | grew; has grown |
| choose | chose; has chosen | hang | hung; has hung |
| cling | clung; has clung | has, have | had; has had |
| creep | crept; has crept | hide | hid; has hidden |
| deal | dealt; has dealt | hold | held; has held |
| dig | dug; has dug | keep | kept; has kept |
| do | did; has done | know | knew; has known |
| draw | drew; has drawn | lay (put) | laid; has laid |
| drink | drank; has drunk | lead | led; has led |

222

| Present | Past; past participle | Present | Past; past participle |
|---------|----------------------|---------|----------------------|
| leave | left; has left | sink | sank; has sunk |
| lend | lent; has lent | sit | sat; has sat |
| lie (down) | lay; has lain | sleep | slept; has slept |
| light | lit; has lit | slide | slid; has slid |
| lose | lost; has lost | sling | slung; has slung |
| make | made; has made | sow | sowed; has sown |
| mean | meant; has meant | speak | spoke; has spoken |
| meet | met; has met | spring | sprang; has sprung |
| prove | proved; has proved or proven | stand | stood; has stood |
| ring | rang; has rung | steal | stole; has stolen |
| ride | rode; has ridden | sting | stung; has stung |
| rise | rose; has risen | stink | stank; has stunk |
| run | ran; has run | strike | struck; has struck |
| say | said; has said | swear | swore; has sworn |
| see | saw; has seen | swing | swung; has swung |
| sell | sold; has sold | take | took; has taken |
| send | sent; has sent | tear | tore; has torn |
| sew | sewed; has sewn | think | thought; has thought |
| shake | shook; has shaken | throw | threw; has thrown |
| shine | shone; has shone | tread | trod; has trodden |
| show | showed; has shown | wear | wore; has worn |
| shrink | shrank; has shrunk | weave | wove; has woven |
| sing | sang; has sung | write | wrote; has written |

A few irregular verbs have the same form for the present, the past and the past participle.

Today I **cut** my hair. Yesterday he **cut** his hair. Already, Toni **has cut** her hair.

Other verbs like *cut* are:

*bet*, *bid* (at buying), *burst*, *cast*, *hit*, *hurt*, *let*, *put*, *read*, *set*, *shed*, *shut*, *slit*, *split*, *wet*

Did you notice two things about each of these words? They each have one syllable and they each end with the letter *t* or *d*.

(Turn the page for more about verbs. →)

a
b
c
d
e
f
g
h
i
j
k
l
m
n
o
p
q
r
s
t
u
v
w
x
y
z

223

Eleven irregular verbs have two possible endings (-*ed* or -*t*) for the past and the past participle. Both endings are correct, but in formal writing -*ed* is used more often.

| Present | Past; past participle | Present | Past; past participle |
|---------|----------------------|---------|----------------------|
| burn | burned or burnt | smell | smelled or smelt |
| dream | dreamed or dreamt | spell | spelled or spelt |
| kneel | kneeled or knelt | spill | spilled or spilt |
| lean | leaned or leant | spoil | spoiled or spoilt |
| leap | leaped or leapt | wrap | wrapped or wrapt |
| learn | learned or learnt | | |

# verse

The word *verse* has two main meanings:

1. Simple rhyming poetry

2. A group of lines with a pattern of rhythm and rhyme that is repeated in the words to a song or poem. This is also called a *stanza*.

For examples of different kinds of verses in poems, see ballad, cautionary tale, couplet, humour, rhyme and rhythm.

**viewpoint** See point of view.

224

# vocabulary

Your *vocabulary* is all the words you know and use when you read, listen, speak and write. The bigger you can make your vocabulary, the better you can communicate.

Your vocabulary grows as you read, listen to speakers, study, watch television reports and documentaries, write, follow hobbies and new interests and research information. Here are some hints for making your vocabulary grow.

### Dictionary

Use a dictionary to check spelling and word meanings.

### Thesaurus

Use a thesaurus to find synonyms and antonyms of words you are using too often in your writing. This is how you gradually learn to use more interesting words.

### Style guide

Use a style guide such as this *Junior Writers Guide* to find out about difficult words. You will find many of these words if you look up confusing words.

### Personal word bank

Develop your own thesaurus and spelling dictionary. You can do this on a computer file or in a project book. For ideas about this, see word bank.

### Word play

Play word games. For ideas, see word play.

# vowels

There are five vowel letters in the alphabet (*a*, *e*, *i*, *o*, *u*). The other twenty-one letters are called *consonants*.

Vowel sounds can be short, such as the *o* in *hop*. The vowels in the following words all have short vowel sounds.

> pat, pet, pit, pot, putt

Vowel sounds can be long, such as the *o* in *hope*. The vowels in the following words all have long vowel sounds.

> late, meet, mean, kite, ski, pie, no, road, flu, flute

The letter *y* can also be used to make vowel sounds.

> m**y**th, sk**y**, carr**y**

The vowel letters *o* and *u* can be used to make consonant sounds.

> The *u* in **U**FO begins with a /y/ sound as in *yellow*.
> The *o* in **o**ne begins with a /w/ sound as in *wonder*.

See also consonants.

**waist** See confusing words: waist, waste.

**wait** See confusing words: wait, weight.

**waste** See confusing words: waist, waste.

**way** See confusing words: way, weigh.

**weak** See confusing words: weak, week.

**weather** See confusing words: weather, whether.

**week** See confusing words: weak, week.

**weigh** See confusing words: way, weigh.

**weight** See confusing words: wait, weight.

**well** See confusing words: good, well.

**we'll** See confusing words: we'll, wheel.

**were** See confusing words: were, where.

**what** See **confusing words**: what, which.

**wheel** See **confusing words**: we'll, wheel.

**where** See **confusing words**: were, where.

**whether** See **confusing words**: weather, whether.

**which** See **confusing words**: what, which and which, witch.

**whole** See **confusing words**: hole, whole.

**win** See **confusing words**: beat, win.

**witch** See **confusing words**: which, witch.

**won** See **confusing words**: one, won.

# word bank

People who write dictionaries collect examples of words in use. They watch how new words come into the language and how old words get new meanings. They keep this information in a *data bank* or *word bank*.

Keeping your own word bank is a good way to improve your vocabulary. It is also a very useful reference when you are writing and looking for rhyming words for a poem, speech verbs for dialogue or more interesting words for descriptions of characters and scenes.

Use a project book or a loose-leaf folder to store interesting words and groups of words you could use in your writing. Loose-leaf folders are useful because you can always add or remove pages when you need to. You could also store words in a word bank file on a computer. Here are some hints.

### Order

List words under headings in *alphabetical order* so you can find them when you need them later. See order.

### Research

Add new words whenever you discover them. This could be when you are solving a problem in your writing or when you are doing spelling activities in class.

### Grouping

Group words that have similar patterns. Some examples might be:

- *parts of speech* (action verbs, collective nouns). See parts of speech.
- *prefixes* (dis-, ex-, -im-, in-, re-, etc) and *suffixes* (-ed, -ing, -ly, -ness, -th, etc). See prefixes and suffixes.
- *rhyming words* (for use in poems, etc). See rhyme.
- *spelling patterns* (*ar*, *ei*, *ght*, *ir*, plurals, silent letters). See spelling.
- *antonyms* and *synonyms* (big, cute, lots, nice, pretty, said, small, etc). See antonyms and synonyms.

# word building

Words can have many forms. *Word building* means changing the form of a word by adding or deleting word parts. You do this so you can use a word in different ways in your writing.

Word building is a way you can find new words to add to your personal word bank.

For more ideas on the ways you can build words, see **affixes**, **plural**, **prefixes**, **root words**, **spelling** and **suffixes**.

# word histories

Most words in our language are very old. Some came from Old English, the language of the very early people of England. They were called *Anglo-Saxons*. Since then, many words have been added to the language. Here are where most of our words come from and how they were invented.

### Old English

The first English words came from Old English. The spelling of some words has changed more than others. This is one reason we have silent letters in words. Here are some examples:

> *among*, *answer*, *between*, *could*, *cow*, *English*, *might*, *holiday*, *knight*, *Monday*, *Saturday*, *should*, *sword*, *Thursday*, *Tuesday*, *two*, *Wednesday*, *who*, *window*, *would*

You can find the story of many of these words if you look up **APPENDIX: WORD HISTORIES**.

### Science and technology

Many new words are invented by scientists and inventors. Scientists often borrow words from the Latin and Greek languages when they need a word to name an invention. Here are some examples:

> *antibiotic*, *astronaut*, *bicycle*, *microscope*, *photograph*, *radio*, *submarine*, *telescope*, *television*

(Turn the page for more about word histories. →)

Here are some modern words that have been added since the invention of the computer.

*CD-ROM, DVD, email, Internet, spell checker, website, word processor*

**Trade and travel**

As the old English explorers travelled, settled in other lands and brought back new foods and things, the names of those things often came from languages in those countries. Here are some examples:

*barbecue, chocolate, coffee, kangaroo, kayak, magazine, potato, shampoo, tea, toboggan*

You can find the story of one of these words if you look up **APPENDIX: WORD HISTORIES**: magazine.

**Word parts**

Many words came from the parts of other words or from people's names. This is a common way of inventing new modern words. Here are some examples:

• **acronyms** (*radar, scuba, TV, UFO*). See acronyms.

• **compound words** (*butterfly, football, sunshine*). See compound words.

• **people's names** (*August, Celsius, Ferris wheel, July*)

• **portmanteau words** (*brunch, motel, smog*). See portmanteau words.

You can find the story of many words and symbols if you go to **APPENDIX: WORD HISTORIES**.

# word play

Word play means having fun with word games. At the same time, people who enjoy word play also become better spellers and develop their vocabulary.

Word play can be exciting because you make discoveries — things you may not have noticed before. For example, look up silent letters and discover a spelling pattern for the silent letter *b*.

Here are some ideas for exploring words. As you make interesting discoveries, you might record them in your personal word bank.

## Mirror words

Some words, phrases and even sentences are spelled the same backwards as they are forwards. It is as if they have a mirror in the middle. The correct name for these words is *palindromes*. Here are some examples:

> *ewe*, *kayak*, *madam*, *pop*, *pup*, *sagas*

## Silent letters

Every letter of the alphabet can be a silent letter. Can you find, for every letter, a word in which it is silent?

## Vowels

How many vowels can you have next to each other?
> t**o**, y**ou**, q**ue**en

Can you find a word with *five* vowels next to each other?

## Word parts (prefixes and suffixes)

How many prefixes and suffixes can you add to one root word? Here is an example:

> *venture*: **ad**venture, **ad**ventur**ous**, **ad**ventur**ously**

**would of** See **confusing words**: could've, could of.

**would've** See **confusing words**: could've, could of.

**write** See **confusing words**: right, write.

# writing process

Professional writers, editors and publishers go through a process of different stages to develop a piece of writing. It helps writers make their meaning clear to their readers. Here is the process an author went through on a writing project.

### Project planning

• **Audience and purpose**

The writer needed to write a short narrative that teaches a lesson to children. He listed the choices of story type: an *allegory*, a *fable*, a *parable* or a *cautionary tale*.

The author chose to write a *cautionary tale*. He would write it as a poem, because there is a tradition of funny cautionary tales being written in this way for children.

• **Research**

The author searched for examples of cautionary verse to make sure that he did not write about a topic or character that already existed. He found poems like 'Matilda, Who Told Lies and Was Burned to Death' by Hilaire Belloc. Now he knew what *not* to use as a topic.

• **Brainstorming ideas**

Here are the author's first notes for ideas on a topic.

*Topics*
*Road safety*
*- crossing the road*
*- wearing seatbelts*
*Health*
*- smoking cigarettes*
*- eating junk food*
*Behaviour*
*- being a bully*
*- being dishonest*

### • Choosing a topic and character

The author chose not to use any of his first ideas, but one note did give him another idea. Instead of the topic *eating junk food*, he decided to focus on what happens to a character if he or she does not eat vegetables. This was because his daughter did not like vegetables.

He chose a boy as a character (so his daughter did not think it was about her). He explored some ideas to plan the events in his story. Here are his notes.

> *1. Intro*
> *- character & problem (won't eat vegies)*
> *2. Problem worsens*
> *- character acts badly (refuses to eat)*
> *3. Crisis*
> *- character in danger (thin as paper?)*
> *4. Resolution*
> *- character disappears (blows away?)*
> *5. Conclusion*
> *- moral (eat vegies or else!)*

The author's notes show that he planned the poem to have five stages. This would mean five verses. These notes tell the author what he must try to write in each verse. He is now ready to write a first draft.

### Drafting

At this stage, the author did not know the name of his character. He did not know exactly how the rhythm and rhyme of his verse would sound. He just wanted to follow his plan and get some ideas down in a rough verse. He could tidy it up later.

(Turn the page to find out what the author did next. →)

a
b
c
d
e
f
g
h
i
j
k
l
m
n
o
p
q
r
s
t
u
v
**w**
x
y
z

The author wrote the first draft of his poem.

---

*Verne Who Avoided Vegetables*
*Verne wouldn't eat potatoes,*
*He wouldn't eat ~~his~~ ^a^ beans~~.~~*
*His parents said, "You'll get really sick,*
*You know just what we mean."*

*But Verne just refused to eat*
*And closed his mouth up tight*
*His parents called the doctor*
*In the midle of the night*

*The doctor tried but sadly failed*
*And Verne, he got much thinner*
*Gradally he faded away*
*He didn't look like a winner.*

*This tale is sad, it brings a tear*
*To know that ~~Verne just passed away~~ poor*
*Verne died.*
*Because he got so thin ~~at last~~ and lean*
*His grave is not to wide.*

*The lesson in this tale is ~~plain~~ clear*
*Potatoes and beans you should eat each day*
*Or you'll end up just like poor Verne*
*And sadly pass away.*

---

Did you notice?
- The author changed a few words as he was writing, and afterwards when he read his draft.
- Some of the lines don't have a regular rhythm.
- There are also some spelling errors.

At this stage, the author had not even noticed the errors. He knew he could tidy them up later. He was thinking more about the ideas in the story.

**Revising**

The author put the draft away for a day. The next morning, he read it again and could see things that did not sound right. He made lists of rhyming words to find other ways to write ideas. He made changes. Then he read it again and made more changes.

This is what it looked like when he showed it to his editor.

> ## The Tale of Larry
> ## Who Wouldn't Eat his Vegetables
> *Larry wouldn't eat his sprouts,*
> *He wouldn't eat a bean.*
> *"You'll get ill," his parents said,*
> *"You'll get all skinny and lean."*
>
> *When vegetables were on his plate,*
> *Larry closed his mouth up tight;*
> *No matter what the doctors did,*
> *He never took a bite.*
>
> *Larry became so thin and frail,*
> *Like a sheet of silver foil,*
> *His parents couldn't give him hugs*
> *For fear that he would spoil.*
>
> *And so I truly tell you all,*
> *It pains me now to say*
> *One day the wind picked Larry up*
> *And blew him clear away.*
>
> *So learn this lesson well, my friends*
> *Eat sprouts and beans each day*
> *Or like poor Larry you'll get thin*
> *Then fade and blow away!*

Did you notice?

- The author changed some of his ideas. As he developed the writing, new ideas came to him.
- The rhythm of the lines is now more regular.
- The spelling errors have been corrected.

(Turn the page to find out what the author did next. →)

a
b
c
d
e
f
g
h
i
j
k
l
m
n
o
p
q
r
s
t
u
v
**w**
x
y
z

### Editing

Most professional writers find it hard to edit their own writing. It is not easy to see all the problems in your own work. Writers need an editor to help them.

First the editors check the **ideas** to see if the story is interesting. They also check that it makes sense. In this example, they would ask, does it do what a cautionary tale is supposed to do? Does it teach a lesson in a humorous way?

Next, the editors check the **style** and **organisation** of the text to see if it is well-written as a poem. In this example, they would check the patterns in the rhythm and the rhyme. They might look for sounds in the words — alliteration for example — to see if it can be improved.

### Proofreading

Finally, the editors check the words to see if the meaning is clear. Do the author's words mean what he thinks they mean? Would the reader understand it? They also check the **capital letters, punctuation** and **spelling**.

The editors discuss all these things with the author. When they agree that the writing is the best they can make it, the poem is published.

### Publishing

Publishing means making the writing available to an audience. It might be published in a newspaper, a book, a magazine or a letter. It might be put on the Internet. It might also be performed as a play or read out loud.

If you want to know how the author's poem about Larry was published, see cautionary tale.

**wrung** See **confusing words**: rung, wrung.

**yew** See **confusing words**: ewe, yew, you.

**you** See **confusing words**: ewe, yew, you.

**your** See **confusing words**: your, you're.

**you're** See **confusing words**: your, you're.

# APPENDIX: WORD HISTORIES

**abbreviation** The word *abbreviation* came from the Latin word *abbreviatio* which meant 'short'.

**acronym** This word comes from two Greek words: *akro* ('at the tip or end') and *onyma* ('name'). An acronym uses letters at the tip or ends of words.

**am (a.m.)** This comes from the Latin words *ante* ('before') and *meridiem* ('midday' or 'noon'). Therefore, *am* means 'before midday'.

**ampersand (&)** School books once listed the alphabet with the symbol & (*and*) after the letter Z. When children chanted the alphabet they would say 'X Y Z and, per se, and'. *Per se* means 'by itself'. They blurred the words 'and per se and' into one word — *ampersand*. This became the name of the symbol &.

**answer** In Old English, the word *andswaru* came from two parts: *and-* ('against') and *swaru* ('to swear' an oath). It meant to swear under oath if you were accused of something. It came to mean 'a reply' to any question. The spelling changed to *answer*. The *w* was kept, but we no longer say it. It became a silent letter.

**April** This word came from *Aprilis*, the name the Ancient Romans gave to the fourth month of the year. Some think that it comes from the Latin word *aperire* ('to open'): April in Rome is spring — the time of year when flowers open.

**@** The @ symbol was invented over one thousand years ago. It was an abbreviation of the ancient Roman word *ad* meaning 'at, to' or 'toward'. Over many years, traders in Europe used the @ symbol to mean 'at a price of'. Later, it was used on an invention called a typewriter. The typewriter keyboard later became the computer keyboard. The @ symbol was used for the first time as part of an email address in 1971.

**August** The eighth month of the year was named after the Roman emperor Augustus.

**autobiography** This word comes from three different Greek words: *auto* ('self'), *bios* ('life') and *graphos* ('write'). When you write the story of your own life, you are writing an autobiography.

**between** The Old English word *betweonum* meant 'by two'. The sound and the spelling of this word slowly changed to *between*. It is still used in an old form sometimes when we say *betwixt and between*. The words *two*, *twice* and *twins* are from the same family.

**biography** This word comes from two different Greek words: *bios* ('life') and *graphos* ('write'). A biography is writing that is about someone's life.

**breakfast** When you are asleep at night, you are not eating. So it is as if you are 'fasting'. Many years ago people thought that the first meal of the day was 'breaking a fast'. So it became known as *breakfast*.

**cereal** The ancient Romans invented this word for the crops they grew (wheat, rye, barley, etc). They named these things after their goddess of agriculture, *Ceres*. Now it means not only the grain that farmers grow but also the breakfast foods made from grain.

**chronological** This word comes from the Greek word *khronos* meaning 'time'. Chronological order means 'in the order of time'.

**cliché** The French word *clicher* imitated the sound made when hot metal was poured into moulds for letters used in printing machines. Printing machines reproduce the same words many times. The word *cliché* came to mean words or phrases that have been repeated over and over again.

**December** To the ancient Romans, December was the tenth month of the year. The Latin word for 'ten' is *decem*. December is our twelfth month because the Romans later added another two months to the year.

238

**dessert** In France and England, people used to clear the table after the main meal. Then bowls of fruit and other sweet foods were brought and people helped themselves. The French word for this was *desservir* from *des-* ('not') and *servir* ('to serve'). It was the course that was 'not served'.

**dollar symbol ($)** An old Mexican-Spanish coin called a *reale* had an image of two pillars with ribbon around them. The ribbon flowed in the shape of an S. The symbol for a dollar ($) was modelled on this — a letter *S* with a pillar running through it. Sometimes it has two vertical lines representing the pillar, but one line is now more common.

*Mexican-Spanish reale coin and diagram of dollar sign taken from its design*

**entrée** This French word means 'entering'. The entrée was a small dish that was the 'entry' to the main meal. However, in America, the word came to mean 'the course that followed the appetiser'. So, if you order an entrée in the UK, Australia, New Zealand and Singapore you will be served a small dish. If you order an entrée in the US, you will be served the main meal.

**February** In the middle of the second month of the year, a region in Italy once had a festival called *februarius*. Our second month is named after this.

**Friday** This word comes from the Old English word *frige-dag* ('Frig's day'). Frig was the old Viking goddess of love.

239

**-gh** In Old English some words like *might* were spelled *miht* or *myht*. After the Normans conquered England in 1066, their writers used their French spelling rules and changed the *yh* to *igh* (*might*, *fight*, *light*, *sight*).

The Normans also changed *h* to *gh* in various other Old English words that had different sounds: *genoh* ('enough'), *toh* ('tough'), *ruh* ('rough'), *theah* ('though'), *thoht* ('thought') and *thurh* ('through', 'thorough'). Sometimes the *gh* was silent, especially before the letter *t*. Sometimes it was given an /f/ sound (*rough*).

**homograph** This word comes from two Greek words: *homos* meaning 'same' and *graphos* meaning 'write'. Homographs are words that are written the same but have different meanings and sounds. Examples are *tear*, *wear*, *wind*, *row*.

**homonym** This word comes from two Greek words: *homos* meaning 'same' and *onoma* meaning 'name'. Homonyms are words that have the same sound or spelling but have different meanings. Examples are *bear*, *bare* and *row*.

**homophone** This word comes from two Greek words: *homos* meaning 'same' and *phone* meaning 'voice, sound'. Homophones are words that have the same sound but different spelling and meanings. Examples are *for*, *four*, *fore*.

**hour** The English took this word from French *heure* but spelled it *hour*. The French do not pronounce the letter *h*. That is why we have a silent letter *h* in this word.

**January** On New Year's Eve people remember the year just passed and look forward to the year ahead. The ancient Romans named this month *Januarius* after *Janus*, a Roman god whose head had two faces — one looking backward and the other looking forward.

240

**June** The ancient Romans named this month after *Juno*, their goddess of marriage. June is summer in Rome — a sunny month to get married.

**July** In old Roman times, the calendar had only ten months. The Roman emperor Julius Caesar changed the calendar by adding two months and inventing the leap year. The seventh month was named after Julius Caesar. His name Julius, in English, is *July*.

**knight** The Old English word *cniht* was pronounced /k-**nik**-tuh/. It meant 'young man' or 'man servant'. Later, its meaning changed to 'soldier'. Then, when men fought battles on behalf of their lord or landowner, they were called *knights*. In modern times the word was used for someone who was honoured by a king or queen for services to the country. All this time, the meaning, the sound and spelling of the word changed. The *-cht* spelling changed to *-ght* and the *k* in *knight* became silent. See also WORD HISTORIES: **-gh**.

**lower case** Years ago, printers kept letters for type in alphabetical order in large, sloping wooden trays called *cases*. The small letters, which the printer had to get more often, were kept in the lower part of the cases, so they were called *lower case*. See **upper case**.

**magazine** This word comes from the old Arabic word *makhazin* meaning 'storehouse'. In 1731, this word was first used to mean 'a publication with articles by various writers'. It was a 'storehouse' of ideas.

**March** The ancient Romans named the third month of the year *Martius*, after *Mars*, their god of war. The French borrowed this word as *Marche*. Then the English borrowed it from French as *March*.

**May** The ancient Romans named this month after *Maia*, their goddess of growth. In Rome, it is spring in May and the flowers bloom and grow.

**Monday** In Old English this word was *monandag* ('moon day') or 'the day of the moon'.

**November** To the ancient Romans, *novembris* was the ninth month of the year. Their word for 'nine' was *novem*. *November* came into English as the name of our eleventh month.

**October** To the ancient Romans, *octobris* was the eighth month of the year. The Latin word for 'eight' is *octo*. So October, which is our tenth month, really means 'eighth month'.

**pm (p.m.)** This comes from the Latin words *post* ('after') and *meridiem* ('midday' or 'noon'). Therefore, *pm* means 'after midday'.

**report** This word comes from two Latin words: *re* ('back') and *portare* ('to carry'). So a report is writing that 'carries back' information.

**RSVP** RSVP is an acronym from the French words *Répondez s'il vous plaît*, which means 'reply if it pleases you' or 'please reply'. It is sometimes written as *R.S.V.P.*

**Saturday** *Saturn* was the ancient Roman god of farming. The Romans named a day *Saturni* after this god. Old English changed this to *Saterdag*. The spelling gradually changed to Saturday in modern English.

**September** The Latin word for 'seven' is *septem*. To the ancient Romans, *september* was the seventh month. *September* is our ninth month because the Romans later invented two more months.

**serial** The ancient Romans used the word *series* to mean 'things connected in a line'. This word came into the English language with the same meaning used by the Romans. The word *serial* (from *series*) was invented to mean stories that were published one part at a time. Charles Dickens wrote serials in a newspaper.

**soup** This word came from the French word *soupe*. It meant 'a piece of bread soaked in liquid'. Later, it came to mean the broth or liquid rather than the bread.

**Sunday** The ancient Romans called this day *dies solis* ('day of the sun'). Old English took this word from the German as *sunnandag*. Later it changed to *Sunday*.

**supper** This word came to English from the Old French word *super*. It meant 'to eat your evening meal'. Later it came to be the name of a small meal eaten late in the evening. The spelling changed to *supper*.

**-tch** Many words with the letters *-tch* were spelled *-icce* in Old English. Over many years, this changed to *-che* or *-cche*. The modern spelling *-tch* happened only a few hundred years ago. *Watch* was *wacca* meaning 'wake'. Later it became *wacche* and then *watch*.

**teddy bear** The teddy bear was named after a US president, Theodore 'Teddy' Roosevelt, who used to hunt bears.

**the** *The* comes from Old English, which had different forms of this word (*se, seo, thæt, thone, thæm* and *thæs*). English became simpler over many years and only one word was used — *the*.

**Thursday** This Old English word was *thunresdag*. Later it became *thórsdagr*, after the Viking god Thor, god of the sky. It is related to the word *thunder*.

**Tuesday** The ancient Germans named this day *tiesdei* after Tiu, their god of war. In Old English this word became *Tiwesdag* and then later, *Tuesday*.

**two** *Two* comes from the Old English word *twa*. The *w* used to be pronounced. Later, the *a* change to an /oo/ sound and the w became silent. We still say the *w* in the words *between*, *twelve*, *twenty*, *twice*, *twin*.

**upper case** Old printers kept capital letters in the top section of the cases holding their type. They were used less than the small letters. They were therefore called *upper-case* letters. See also lower case.

**volt** The word *volt*, a measure of electricity, comes from the name of an Italian scientist, Alessandro Volta, who improved batteries.

**Wednesday** The ancient Vikings named days after gods and bodies in the solar system. They named Wednesday after Odin, their chief god. In Old English, Odin was known as *Woden*, so this word became *Wodnesdag*. The spelling was changed to *Wednesday*. The first letter *d* used to be spoken.